AF493095

THE LOUISVILLE REVIEW

SUMMER 2023

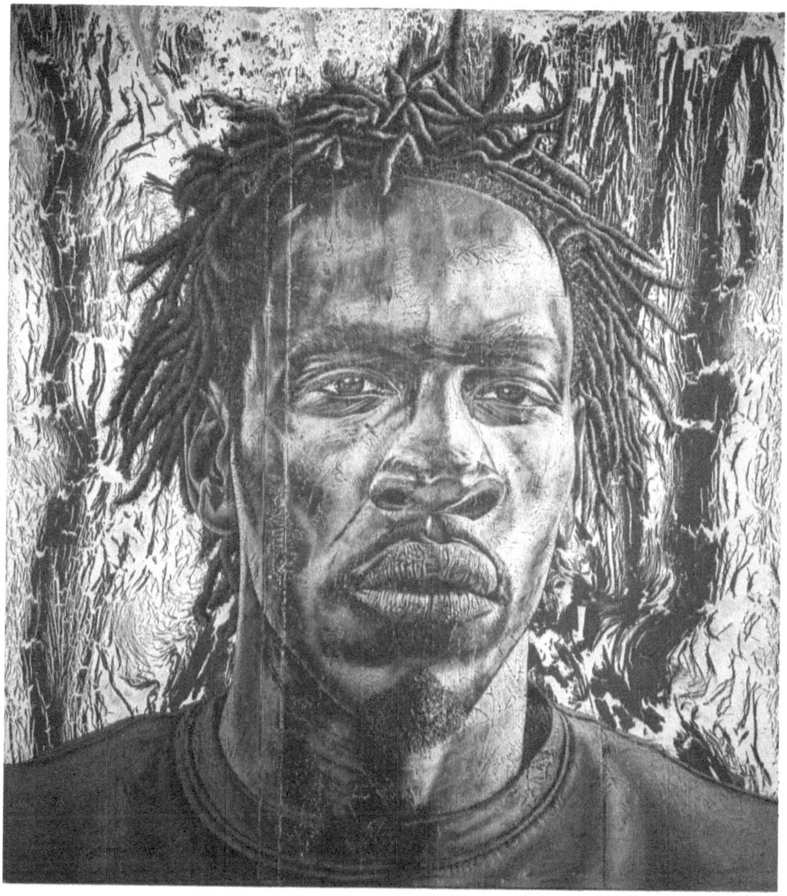

Alfred Conteh, *Aaron*

93

The Louisville Review

Editor	Sena Jeter Naslund
Associate Editor	Flora K. Schildknecht
Managing Editor	Amy Foos Kapoor
Guest Poetry Editors	Greg Pape, Tammy Ramsey
Guest Fiction Editor	Juyanne James
Cornerstone Editor	Betsy Woods
Technical Director	Ron Schildknecht
Financial Director	John Morgan

TLR publishes two volumes each year. Visit our website for complete guidelines, back issues, subscriptions, and more: www.louisvillereview.org.

Like us on Facebook for up to date information about each issue, news on contributors, etc.: www.facebook.com/TheLouisvilleReview. Follow us on Twitter @TheLouRev.

Questions? Please note our email and mailing addresses:

managingeditor@louisvillereview.org

The Louisville Review Corp.
1436 St. James Court #1
Louisville, Kentucky 40208

This issue: $10 ppd
Sample copy: $5 ppd
Subscriptions: One year, $18; two years, $36; three years, $54 plus $2 shipping
Subscribers outside the United States please add $35/year for shipping.

Text and cover printed in the United States.
Cover and interior design by Jonathan Weinert.

Cover artwork: Alfred Conteh, *Aaron*, 2018. Acrylic, atomized steel dust, and soil on canvas. Courtesy of the Collection of Laura Lee Brown and Steve Wilson, 21c Museum Hotels. Photographed by Ron Schildknecht.

The Louisville Review is a not-for-profit publication.
The Louisville Review Corporation is a member of the Community of Literary Magazines and Presses.

Associate Editor's Note

For the cover of this issue of *The Louisville Review* we are thrilled
to feature **Alfred Conteh**'s painting *Aaron*. Conteh's painting
appears courtesy of the collection of Laura Lee Brown and Steve
Wilson's 21c Museum Hotels, a longtime partner with Spalding
University's Sena Jeter Naslund-Karen Mann Graduate School of
Writing and *The Louisville Review* in producing Voice & Vision, an
annual summer reading series in Louisville coordinated by *TLR*'s
Managing Editor, Amy Foos Kapoor. The essay "Portraiture, Inside
and Out: Alfred Conteh's *Aaron*," by 21c Chief Curator and Museum
Director **Alice Gray Stites**, sheds light on the ways in which Conteh
aesthetically addresses the structural inequalities Black communities
face, while asserting the power and resilience of those communities
through scale, material, and engagement with the art historical cannon.

Poems by Rosa Nevadovska (1890-1971) open this issue, both in the
original Yiddish text—a first for *TLR*—and in English translation
by **Merle L. Bachman**. These poems appear in *Still Glimmering:
Selections from the Poetry of Rosa Nevadovska*, Bachman's forthcoming
collection of Nevadovska's poems in translation from Ben Yehuda Press;
Bachman's "Translator's Note" shares something of Nevadovska's own
life story.

Over the years *The Louisville Review* has been honored to publish
the poetry of the late Annette Allen, and in this issue, we are pleased
to include **Mary Elizabeth Pope**'s poems selected by Kentucky Poet
Laureate Maureen Morehead for the University of Louisville's Annette
Allen Poetry Prize.

Reading this issue of *TLR*, I'm once again delighted by the range of
voices and of subjects engaged: From an exploration of the too-often-
hidden contributions of Black distillers of Kentucky bourbon, in
Kentucky Poet Laureate **Frank X Walker**'s poem, "Masta d' Steala," to a

speculative view of a not-so-distant future deeply impacted by climate catastrophe in **J. D. Strunk**'s short story "Tokyo, 2031," to human and animal encounters in the poems "When Otters Crossed Penang Road" by Singaporean writer **Verena Tay** and "I Brake for Butterflies" by **Amy Foos Kapoor**, to an assertion of resilience and vibrance in advanced age in **Alice Bingham Gorman**'s poem "The House of Eighty," *TLR #93* presents readers with a wonderfully varied range of human experience.

With this 93rd issue, we recognize five issues of the new *TLR*, now fully independent after generous university sponsorship over past years. Supported first by the University of Louisville and then by Spalding University, *The Louisville Review* was founded in 1976 by Editor Sena Jeter Naslund, along with two undergraduate students, Bonnie Cherry and Tom Willett, at the University of Louisville. For over 45 years *TLR* has continuously published both new and established writers, a mission we are proud to continue today.

This January, *The Louisville Review* will open submissions for our first **National Poetry Book Contest** as an independent literary journal. Thanks to essential support from the Snowy Owl Foundation, the contest will provide publication of a first book of poetry from *The Louisville Review*'s Fleur-de-Lis Press.

The work we do at *TLR* would not be possible without the vital contributions of our guest editors for each issue, and I extend our heartfelt thanks to our guest poetry editors, who, along with myself, selected the poetry for this issue of *TLR*:

Greg Pape is the author of *Four Swans, Animal Time, American Flamingo,* and several other books. His new book of poems, *A Field of First Things,* will be out in November from Accents Publishing. He served as Montana Poet Laureate 2007 to 2009. Professor Emeritus at University of Montana, he teaches in the MFA program at Spalding University's Naslund-Mann School of Writing.

Tammy Ramsey's poems have appeared in *Kentucky's Twelve Days of Christmas, New Growth: Recent Kentucky Writings, The Heartland Review, and The Louisville Review*. Ramsey earned an MA in English from the University of Kentucky and an MFA in writing from Spalding University. She taught English and journalism at several Kentucky colleges and universities and worked as a free-lance copy editor and writer for *The Lexington Herald-Leader*.

Likewise, I must extend our deep gratitude to our guest fiction editor, who along with Editor Sena Jeter Naslund selected the fiction for this issue:

Juyanne James is an Associate Professor of English at the University of Holy Cross, New Orleans, Louisiana and Adjunct Professor of Creative Nonfiction at the University of New Orleans. She is the author of *The Persimmon Trail and Other Stories* (Chin Music Press, 2015), her debut collection of seventeen stories in which she interprets the African American experience in Louisiana, as well as *Table Scraps and Other Essays* (Resource Publishers, 2019), a memoir in essays about growing up in a troubled home. Her stories and essays have been published in journals, such as *The Louisville Review, Mythium, Bayou Magazine, Eleven Eleven, Thrice, Ponder Review, Xavier Review*, and included in the anthologies *New Stories from the South: 2009* (Algonquin) and *Something in the Water: 20 Louisiana Stories* (Portals Press, 2011). Her essay "Table Scraps" was a notable essay in *The Best American Essays 2014* and "You Don't Know Me, Child" was a featured story in New York's *Symphony Space Selected Shorts*.

And many thanks to **Betsy Woods** for her continued service as Editor of Cornerstone, *The Louisville Review*'s section of poetry by young writers in grades K-12.

—Flora K. Schildknecht, Associate Editor

Table of Contents

Poetry

Nonfiction

Fiction

Cornerstone

Poetry

Rosa Nevadovska

פֿאַר נאַכט

איך האָב געזען די זון דורך ווינטערדיקע ביימער,
דורך דעם געפֿלעכט פֿון הוילע שוואַרצע צווייגן.
די פֿיאָלעט־פֿאַרבן האָבן אויף אַ שפֿראַך געהיימער
גערעדט צו מיר די שפֿראַך פֿון טיפֿעניש און שווייגן.

איך בין געגאַנגען דורך די שטילע ווינטערדיקע גערטנער.
די זון האָט זיך געזעצט שוין אין די לעצטע רגעס.
געטראַכט האָב איך פֿון דיר און פֿון די בלויע ערטער,
און אַלץ האָט אויסגעזען בלויז ווי אַן אָנדייַט און אַ רמז.

פֿאַרגאַנגען איז די זון, און אַלץ אַרום איז גרוי געוואָרן,
דער מערבֿ האָט געטונקלט און די פֿאַרבן אויסגעלאָשן.
און יענע רגע האָט געבראַכט צו מיר פֿון ווייַטע יאָרן
דייַן פּנים, דייַנע אויגן און דייַן לשון.

Dusk

I saw the sun through wintry trees,
Through the lattice of naked black boughs.
Violet colors spoke to me of depths
And stillness in a secret tongue.

I walked through the quiet winter gardens.
Minutes earlier, the sun had set.
I thought of you and blue, far-off places and all
Around me I saw signs, clues.

The sun had gone, leaving only gray;
The west was dark, all colors subdued.
And that moment brought to me your face,
From distant years—your eyes, and your language.

from the forthcoming collection *Still Glimmering: Selections from the Poetry of Rosa Nevadovska*, translated from the Yiddish by Merle L. Bachman

Rosa Nevadovska

אַזוי פֿיל וואַרעמע ווערטער

אַזוי פֿיל וואַרעמע ווערטער
אין קאַלטע אויערן גערעדט.
אַזוי פֿיל פֿרעמדע ערטער
מיט אייגענעם לעבן באַלעבט.

און לאַנג, אַזוי לאַנג געגאַנגען
אַליין אויפֿן ליכטיקן וועג,
מיט אָטעם אין מיַינע געזאַנגען
געשטיגן אַליין אויף די טרעפּ.

דעם וואַרעמען אָטעם פֿון האָפֿן
געהויכט אויף אַ פֿראָסטיקער נאַכט,
און וועמען האָב איך דאָרט געטראָפֿן?
ס׳האָט קיינער אויף מיר ניט געוואַרט.

So Many Words

So many warm words
Spoken into cold ears.
So many strange places
Humming with their own life.

And long had I gone, so long,
On my own on a bright path,
Filling my lungs with song,
Climbing alone up the stairs.

That warm breath of hope
When I got to the top,
Exhaled on a frosty night—
No one awaited me there.

from the forthcoming collection *Still Glimmering: Selections from the Poetry of Rosa Nevadovska*, translated from the Yiddish by Merle L. Bachman

Rosa Nevadovska

ווי אַ בין

ווי אַ בין צו בלום צוגעפֿאַלן—
אַזוי טרינק איך פֿון דײַן שיינקייט, דרום.
בײַ טאָג מיך זוניקן די שטראַלן,
בײַ נאַכט—מיך בלוייקט די לבֿנה.

איך רייד זיך דורך מיט די ווײַטע שטערן—
זיי בלישטשען פֿון די הימל־געצעלטן.
רפֿואהדיק וויין איך אויס מײַנע טרערן
אין באַגעגעניש מיט אַנדערע וועלטן.

Like a Bee

The way a bee throws itself at a flower—
That's how I drink from your beauty, oh south.
By day the sun's rays gild me,
By night—I'm blued by the moon.

I talk things through with the distant stars
That sparkle from heaven's tents.
How healing it is, to cry out my tears
In encounters with other worlds.

from the forthcoming collection *Still Glimmering: Selections from the Poetry of Rosa Nevadovska*, translated from the Yiddish by Merle L. Bachman

Rosa Nevadovska

בענקשאַפֿט

ווי שטיל דאָ איז! איך דאַרף ניט קיינעם היַינט.
אַרום מיר בערג—זיי שטײַגן העכער הימל.
פֿון באַרג און ווײַטקייט בין איך איצט אַ פֿרײַנד,
און צווישן זיי און מיר—אַ זילבערדרימל.

אַן אָדלער טראָגט זיך אין די הייכן פֿרײַ.
נעם מיך, אָדלער, אין דײַן וועג דעם ווײַטן!
פֿון דאָרט וועל איך די וועלט דערזען אויף ס׳נײַ—
און אפֿשר אויף אַ פֿויגל זיך פֿאַרבײַטן.

און אפֿשר—אפֿשר אויך אַן אָדלער זײַן,
זיך טראָגן העכער, דאָס האַרץ פֿון זון באַקוקן.
מײַן בלוט וועט ווערן טונקל־רויטער ווײַן—
און פֿליגל וועלן וואַקסן אויף מײַן רוקן.

Yearning

How quiet it is! I need no one today.
Mountains surround me—rising to highest heaven.
I am a friend of mountains now, and distance,
And a wisp of silver thread connects us.

High up drifts an eagle, freely—
Take me, eagle, on your far-off journey!
From there, I'll glimpse the world anew—
Taking on a bird's view.

And maybe—I'll become an eagle, too,
Soaring higher, to see the sun's heart.
My veins will run dark with wine
And from my back, wings will part.

from the forthcoming collection *Still Glimmering: Selections from the Poetry of Rosa Nevadovska*, translated from the Yiddish by Merle L. Bachman

Alice Bingham Gorman

The House of Eighty

From this threshold,
where I stand firm,
I wonder

if I am visible
through the windows
of my eyes.

Can you see
the many rooms?
Can you tell

that nothing
has been lost,
everything

has been used,
and a few things
transformed?

Do you see
the light in my living room
still shines—

and I am still at home?

Verena Tay

Dying

the stylist lifts, lets fall, proclaiming judgement
on white against black: "you should dye."
mindless before authority, i submit.
thus begins a twenty-five-year sentence
imprisoning honest age.

condemned behind youthful bars,
my body riots, roams routes different
from where will prefers to remain.
week by week, month on month, year after year,
quietly, black becomes grey, grey becomes white,
until one day, a mirrored snow head
screams at black remains: "you should die!"

why do we linger at the start
when the journey ahead is what life's all about?
there's nothing wrong with white.
cool as cotton, unlike youth's scratchy polyester,
it's merely a signpost towards the end we must reach,
a badge, reflecting wisdom gained along the way.
so why remain at the beginning and die a dark-haired babe?
instead of mourning, let's thrash that jail,
flaunt our souvenirs, and party till the lights go out.

Verena Tay

When Otters Crossed Penang Road

green opposite : impossible goal
bus-car-van-trunk-rush-by
a-man-made-river

fortunate us : jungle courtesy exists
at red—for ten seconds—
stillness absolute

time to cross : as one family
we ripple, undulate
grey-brown waves : bank to bank

thank Great Lutrinae!
humans call us kawaii
they'd run us over if we'd been rats

now we sunbathe
on shaded sidewalks
fish—anyone?

Amy Foos Kapoor

I Brake for Butterflies

Driving slowly up
the steep mountain
around winding curves—

a kaleidoscope of monarchs
flutters
their gentle wings—

a delicate blur of orange and black
flitters
through the air

careful
not to hit
angelic beings

I tap my foot
on the brake
slowing down

Full Stop.

glorious
butterflies
flit and flutter

across the rocky road

frolicking along
the blue sky

drifting into
the forest

and away

Mary Elizabeth Pope

To Echo the Electric Lines of a House

My pottery teacher sat down at the wheel in a low chair with a student

today and just talked about what it's like to throw a bowl, to pull clay

as if to never touch it, to build a lip, a wall. She asked the student

to hang the air, palm the air, like a stop sign; and set her palm to push

against the student's, a slight touch—to know the resistance of energy

meeting, the tension, the pulling-away and pressing at the same time.

This is how a flat fist of earth moves into the body of a house and makes

something useful. It's that she wasn't afraid to sit with her, beside her, and say:

Hey this is a hard thing, let me show you how it feels to own it.

It's that she saw a need and filled it with her presence.

Winner of the 2022 Annette Allen Poetry Prize, 2011-12 Kentucky Poet
Laureate Maureen Morehead, Judge

Mary Elizabeth Pope

Bedouin

I hold the magenta scarf woven from camel
locks, lace of sun and rose,
a note from the woman near the desert
of Wadi Rum

in Jordan.
My sister floats in the salt of the Dead Sea
and mails the scarf. Call it field work.
My sister knows about death,

the smell of death, old heart of a transplant
removed from the incision
of a chest woven shut.
If I could tell you one thing about Art

it's that you know nothing
until paying the Bedouin woman a Jordanian Dinar
for the story woven into her
in dreams where Jesus woke the water

after her child was given a new heart.
And was brought back
to life. What do the framed plaques offer
residing within the buildings?

My sister places
an artifact from the salt,
sanded hijabs, descent
from a camel at the threshold of Petra.

What museum wants this scarf,
who will pay an ample sum,
do you want the heart
plucked from the chest of my sister's son

to house in the wing of the body
in the museum? Do you want an Xray
of my daughter's spine
fusion lifted from her crushing lungs

by bone to study
on the dissecting table,
refund of my plane ticket
to Tel Aviv to meet her, time in the waiting

rooms of recovery
as proof of an absence.
What is the worth of a scarf
in the desert

by the Wadi Rum—
is it more valuable to find her
resting on the edge of the river
captured in the sepia

of a photograph—
will you pay her for her labor,
will you track her down
before you frame it,

before naming her, naming the scarf:
Artifact #41
to hang in your book,
in the wing of refugee

to offer objections of her worth,
knowing that you'll never weave a scarf
from the hair of a camel on the Wadi Rum.
Never own it, never touch it, never wear it.

Never find her again in that same light.

Winner of the 2022 Annette Allen Poetry Prize, 2011-12 Kentucky Poet Laureate
Maureen Morehead, Judge

Rolly Kent

My Parents in the City of Light

After they died, they arrived in Paris.
They had always wanted to see the sights,
but there was only enough time to seek out
a distant relative of ours in one of
the outer arrondissements. Monsieur Dumont
(that was his name) was unsurprised to see them,
since he expected such visits from obscure
kin like my parents, who came before him with
their last rays of selfhood. My parents had heard
he was skilled at correcting the past; *non*,
M. Dumont said in very simple French,
this was beyond what a mere *bricoleur*
like him was allowed; for this, they needed
someone more skilled than a handyman.
What M. Dumont could do was help them
vacate the space which they were so
accustomed to they couldn't see that they'd
left it filled with disappointment. He explained
why we expect more from life than we receive,
and why, to give itself, life needs more than
just our one body, or our little world—but here
he saw his guests didn't really understand.
So he tried to say it again as best he could
in English. My parents nodded as if they had
suspected as much, but M. Dumont spoke
with such a heavy accent they hadn't
grasped a word he said. They sat for a while
in that tiny front room holding hands
before they let go of each other and became
part of a knowledge we imagine some day
finding in a book, a city, or a face we love.

Rolly Kent

Rhode Island

We're standing like men at their urinals
should, keeping porcelain between us,
when Andy announces his prostate's
the size of Rhode Island. Before I can boast
mine is Delaware, a youth slides into
the empty stall, smug as the kid who ditched
U.S. Geography. We won't quiz him.
What states he doesn't know will still be there
to greet him: Some days it will be Connecticut
with its throbbing rivers, some days big-bellied
Ohio, or Wyoming with its yawning, yellow
plains. Young man, welcome! Stand with us
shoulder to shoulder, slacker and the slacked,
our backs against the world! Join us, unafraid
to gaze into the white and cherry-scented
abyss or upwards where the cracks in heaven are
and God leaked into the ceiling. For men never
know where divinity may find them. Be ready,
one hand free on your hip. But humble,
mindful to zip, and when finished, think of
Rhode Island ceaselessly pounded by ocean,
like the self, ever renewing, onward
flowing towards Providence, its capital.

Debra Kang Dean

Postcards in the Style of Renku

after Hejira

between late night and early morning
    roused you pressed into me as wind
to cool the fire burning within
    je ne regrette rien   no

        no regrets

    fresh air pouring through an open window
  and I   westbound between the rear-view
    and the car's shadow   a widow turned runaway

        *

wandering once-familiar blocks   an old story
    these fronts wrecked and frozen   amid the rubble
a cascade of footfalls   one gait prying loose a memory:
    I don't like you   not your money I mean

      but *you*

    weaving and dodging through the suburb's grid—
  I hear tell the latest of bored rollerbladers
    hitching themselves to eighteen wheelers

      to get their kicks

points of departure these crumbling infrastructures
    frost heaves   rumble strips   deer in the headlights
    ground notes lifting above one voice

love-vexed   an instrument   sometimes a helix
sometimes a hex   a seemingly inevitable

touch and go

clouds and rain   then the sky clearing
        somewhat   somewhat dispelling illusions—
where a bridge collapsed   a detour
        into terrain   circling out of the familiar

and here I am

    dressing to suit the weather and of course black
    pearls—they were his eyes you know—*cold & passionate*
    this constant urge to skate on thin ice

*

the countervailing desire after a while
        lying alone in muted blue light:
of a shared warm bed   of a shared vision's
        depth of the field—already there and not

yet there

    where roads converge and diverge
    between the open plains and the wild sea
        over and back over and out
            out and away

Brian Turner

Los Angeles

It's one of those things I have little memory of—
my half brother, a toddler, floating facedown
in the pool, his lips turned an awful shade of blue.
Around us, the city slept on. A coastal fog rolled in
as seagulls wheeled above, crying out in hunger.
I'm told I saved him by climbing a flight of stairs
to wake my exhausted young mother, a go-go dancer
at a club in North Hollywood. What I remember
are the Crown Royal bags full of her nightly tips,
the snare drum I'd bang along to Iron Butterfly,
drumming my heart out to that 2 ½-minute solo
on the extended jam of "In-A-Gadda-Da-Vida,"
the Summer of Love playing in the background.
My little brother was raised by his own father
in Buena Park, while our mother returned with me
to the San Joaquin Valley. He lived with us once
for a year, when he was a 6th grader, setting fire
to the dead grasslands around us, stealing a pistol
from the neighbor's house, discharging a shotgun
into the furniture, and chasing Ronald McCree
with a can of hair spray and a lighter improvised
into a blowtorch. The years would not be kind to him.
He spent a couple of them under the California
Youth Authority. Then a series of halfway houses.
A failed marriage. His own kids, my niece and nephews,
doing time now, one of them on the run after an incident
with a weapon and a stolen car. And he's back in Fresno
now, living on the streets, with pills and crystal meth
searing through his veins. And I have to wonder
who is he, this brother of mine. Because that little boy

floating in the pool long ago, he never really made it out,
a part of him died right there in the water, and I didn't
save him at all, and I haven't, to this day, ever really met
the man I call my little brother, that blue-lipped child
who was a toddler when he fell in, only 14 months
younger than me, and what the hell did we know
about water, or air, or drowning, or anything at all.

Brian Turner

The Sweetest Way to Drown

In the pool, two lovers float on inflatable rafts
as if still in bed from the night before, oblivious
to everything around them. And I am only nine,
but even I know when a promise is being made,
a bond that will carry them through the decades
ahead, lean times when welding and tending bar
won't always be enough, and later, too, when a surgeon
wires his heart back together, and when the car crash
shatters vertebrae in her neck. How cautious and tender
they'll be in the shower then, tracing the sutured furrow
that holds him together before guiding liquid soap
between the bars of the halo and down through
the auburn channels of her hair. These things
we can share. What it's like to watch your parents
fall in love. As they did poolside that summer's day.
Their friends drinking since noon and laughing
in the grass by the smoking grill, hard liquor
poured into tumblers of ice as they told stories
about hospitals and jail and weekends and work,
and mostly their stories were just about being
alive in times like these. And that's when Old Man
Kelman, drunk as usual and slurring about his service
on the HMS Hood, leaned over with his dead eyes
and his dead breath to startle me, then turned away
just as my heels caught the concrete lip of the pool
and I wheeled backwards through the afternoon light—
falling wordless through the ether, a frightened little boy
who didn't know how to swim, though the water
gathered me in its blue embrace, otherworldly,
cold and clear, spangled with the American Bicentennial

that would cast fireworks over Fresno that night.
And in that moment, I couldn't see the rescue coming—
my Uncle Paul, fully-dressed, diving headfirst into the air
at the far end of the pool. I simply watched the number 9
rise higher and higher as I sank towards my own shadow,
which lay on the bottom alongside the shadows cast down
by my mother and the man who would become my father.
And I didn't panic as I sank. My thoughts seemed to mirror
the water. That clarity. I remember it well. It was all so tranquil.
I miss it still. The two lovers drifting side by side, their silhouettes
merging into one. And I held my breath for as long as I could.
And I watched the two of them as they disappeared into the sun.

Frank X Walker

Masta d' Steala

The truth about the history of bourbon
especially, when *they* say the secret
came from an "old family recipe,"
is that ol' Grand Dad, likely owned the cook.

So it ain't no different than colonels laying claim
to discovering the "thirteen herbs and spices"
that make the yardbird "finger licking good"
or Christopher   columbusing.

Jack Daniel told the truth about the African
source of the double filtration process,
but in Kentucky they give all the credit
to limestone in the water, before acknowledging
the Black hands of a cook or a cooper.

Truth is, somebody skilled enough to regulate
temperatures over an open fire, somebody who
knew cornmeal from cracked corn or grits,
and all about cooking   in vats and giant pots,

a body who knew how many heirloom kernels
it took to plant forty acres and feed the mule,
how many bushels to set aside as seed

fingers that knew hoe & plow, plant & grow,
put mineral oil on the silk to stop the corn ear worm,
knew how many stalks to let dry in the field
to be picked & husked after the silk turned brown.

Not shuck and jive, but shuck & shell—by hand,
to be ground or milled, barreled, shipped, and sold,
before using the cobs for kindling, dolls or pipes
or for their private business in the outhouse.

A body who knew how much six-row barley
and when to add it,
to coax starch to fermentable sugars,
so that fruit or grain could be worshipped
as beer or wine on the way to being born again
as brandy or whiskey (bourbon in the bluegrass)

Every body knew a body with no land, no power,
no voice, no control, had   no say
over who say who is the master   distiller.

Mary Makofske

Bomb Squad Detonates Live Civil War Cannonball Found in Maryland

This cannonball has a long history.
Who knows how many men it targeted,
or whether they wore blue or gray.
For more than a century and a half
it rested undisturbed as a dormant seed.
Weeds can do that, too, spring
to life when conditions are right, also
desert flowering plants ignited by rain
to explode blood red, pus yellow,
gangrene purple or blue. Weapon
sleeping through other wars, stock market's
roller coaster, the waxing and waning
of attention to the conflict it survived.

Still potent with gunpowder the Chinese
invented, first for fireworks, starbursts
in the night sky celebrating one new year
after another, celebrating the birth
of our nation, reminder of the bombs
bursting in air, as this one could have,
like the buried myths and animosities
that keep turning up. We need a bomb
squad with nimble hands and minds to defuse
our volatile national amnesia, our explosive
anger and hatred. Just blowing them up
scatters shrapnel that may strike us,
no matter how far from them we stand.

Kevin Boyle

Two Women of Havana

"and by and by a cloud takes all away"

I'm remembering
unclearly the street
in Old Havana,
away from the parades
of folks on stilts
panhandling, busking
just beyond plainclothes police
checking documents for permission
to be anywhere, the sun
a hot hand
pressing down on heads,
there by my hotel
where Cubans could
not sleep or stay, in the shade
of the building and palms,
two women—how
did we meet?— began to
unfold a simple plan of luxury
I would help, please, sir.
I did not ask what's
in it for me, but agreed to meet
at three in this same shade,
perhaps more if clouds came,
while that night, alone, I imagined
meeting them dressed
in their finest, which would not be
fine, and they might walk
with me along the Malacon
allowing me to kiss one

after another, but the next day
in the same July heat, I brought
the two bars as planned
to the shade, and presented
one by one from my now
floral pockets the two hotel
soaps, unlike any other soap
in the streets of La Habana,
and they held them
to their noses, took a deep breath
in and smiled, thanking me
and smiling, smiling. You have
no idea, one said. No idea,
the other said. When I bathe
I will think of you. No, I said,
I will think of you, please.
They placed the soaps
beneath their blouses in case
of police since begging was
against the law, but you weren't
begging, I insisted. It was my
pleasure, my gift, and they walked
toward the ruined street
where my bicycle-rickshaw driver
two days before
offered me cigars or women,
either one, my friend, either one
for a good man, a kind American.

Derek Otsuji

Porch Swing at Evening

I like to sit and watch the world go by
she said, in a quiet dreamy sort of mood,
talking to herself, though aware I stood
there, like a shadow, come to say goodbye.
It was less declaration than a sigh
that issued from her lips, like when we brood
out loud over some truth we've understood,
feel compelled to speak, yet wonder why.
Beside her on the green porch swing I watched
a lone horse on the opposing hill
graze lazily on, to his own sweet will. . .
as if the gathering hours were his own.
The sky bruised, faded to a lilac swatch.
An egret sailed, white as her hair now shone.

Derek Otsuji

Redemption

On the park lawn—
     aluminum, plastic
     in separate piles.

When he gets around
     to sorting the glass,
     he tosses green bottles

with the green,
     brown bottles with
     the brown. Clink, clink.

Each pile goes
     into a separate
     bag, distended

pouches with orange
     ties. He does not
     pause or look up

from his work,
     his face, a furnace
     that will melt these

down, make them
     into new bottles
     for new beer.

A future he can
     drink to. Clink,
     clink, clink.

By dint of work
        he climbs out
        from the pit. The sun

peeps from behind
        blind buildings. He
        reloads his rattling cart

with the bags.

Marin Bodakov

Unmailed Letter

I went to the executioner's house,
which utilizes the last surviving partition of the fortress's wall.
You know, those stones were pillaged
so we could build spacious mansions,
so you could discuss with the steward the menu for the inaugural ball,
how best to light the stoves,
so I could calculate the next business deal while playing solitaire
and waiting for dinner.
By the way, the executioner turned out to be a really nice man,
I stayed all day to pester him.
I didn't allow him to get any work done,
I am yet to leave.

Translated from the Bulgarian by Katerina Stoykova

Christopher Buckley

All Hallows

I look up
        to the Japanese maple—
its bruise-red leaves
            lifting in a gust
like song notes
         on the white-
washed afternoon. . . .
            Sunlight
brazing the mist,
        I'm close to forgetting
another year . . .
         hummingbirds blurring
about the feeders,
          disappearing south.
Neighbor's persimmons,
           like a gold orrery,
are suspended
        over a brown lawn, over
my two grey cats,
        my grey heart . . .
I offer up
        a threadbare hope for what
I haven't understood
        or managed to say, exactly,
and push it gently seaward
            on the visible fog
of my breath.
       Perhaps it's enough
              to just gaze
about the yard, and,
        like my cats, like the bees,

praise everything

                  as long as it lasts. . . .
All I need is

           more time, an extension of that
knotted invisible string,

                growing shorter
again, here, where starlings

                  and finches
balance

        on phone lines

                  above the shadow-
heavy roofs,

        like me, waiting for the last
instructions of the light. . . .

Lennie Hay

Resurrection

I hug him to my chest,
a silent tree trunk
that stands watch
through nights
and welcomes me at dawn.

I strum ridges of his armor
molded to his chest,
almost hear his ancient war cry.

I bend my legs to hoist him
from a pedestal behind the couch,
move him into full view
in hopes that light
will give him voice.

A general's strength
should flow unimpeded,
to carry 8000 loyal warriors
into the 21st century.

I hoped Xian warriors
would teach me my history—
imperial excess,
craftsmanship,
ancestor worship—
so I had him shipped
to my home.

Umber figure, armor and tunic
fitted on his compact body
under a helmeted,
bearded head   remains silent,
as my father was.
Neither tells tales
from underground.

Unearthed from fields,
the general was born again
in a museum market,
then shipped to Tampa.

I place him in the room's
most auspicious position
where I watch his closed lips,
watch him   watch me.

Lennie Hay

Burial Ground

Mother swept away
remorseless beach sand
during her bright years,
knew it would return
to our cottage,
a sunny chapel,
but swept it anyway.
Such grit
would not be expelled,
nor would crusted sandals,
salty t-shirts,
family ghosts.

Now I'm as old as Mother
was when she swept
our residue.
I walk
on ancient crushed quartz,
Florida sand mixed
with bits of discarded
fish bones and skin
sloughed from our feet
making a beach gumbo
that stinks of dead seaweed
and memory.

Some days the beach tickles,
smooth and damp
as a child's extended tongue;
then changes and scours,

rippled and ridged
as a steel washboard.

This quartz washed down
from tired mountains
and cold streams
mingles with pieces
of plastic shovels and buckets,
broken boogie boards
scraps of forgotten towels
threads of family secrets.

Once my love and I stalked
forgiveness
after a hail of wounding words,
found a firm bed of sand
where we made love
hidden in night shadows.

Today in full sun
a sprawling sculpture stands—
moat and castle preserved
above the high tide line.
A bleached seabean stem
tops the tower,
a finger rising
from the grave.

Peter Kent

John Lennon's Alive

He lives in New Hampshire,
where he teaches geology as an adjunct professor
and works part-time at the lodge where your grandfather
spent years investing energy into the black hole
of poetry. While a child, John lost an eye to measles,
and it's unclear if he's ever picked up a guitar.
A famous name is an odd birthmark. Unlike
the young bear who visited the lodge one spring,
meandering through the parking lot and down
to the pond, it matters what we're called. I called
the bear Claude, after a Canadian gentleman who coached
the Boston Bruins. Though the bear didn't care
how amused I was by this charade of cleverness.
John loves to watch hockey, and I'd find him sometimes
in the basement with his laptop set on top of a washing machine,
streaming classic games from past Stanley Cup finals
while working out on his homemade stair stepper.
John Lennon of New Hampshire, enjoying life
in obscurity—trapped now in this poem's
obscure amber, so that you might be aware
of his existence, this gentle man
with the eminent moniker, this mayfly
skimming across eternity's dark surface.

Frances Schenkkan

Eartha Kitt

What we hear is not only sound,
it's memory—LBJ's twang,
my father's curled lip *N*—

What did Lady Bird silently
label her guest? Imagine, Ms. Kitt
arriving at the White House lunch

with other ladies to discuss youth violence
and she lashes out about Vietnam,
about young men so alienated

"they rebel in the streets."
Lady Bird's voice trembled and tears
welled up, not from sympathy.

Within weeks, most of Kitt's appearances
were cancelled. Her acting career floundered.
Years later she learned the President

had ordered the CIA to investigate her.
Don't you dare make Bird cry like that,
don't you dare criticize her husband's war,

not when the first lady was in Harlem
planting trees, and wildflowers would soon
come up all along the highways of America.

Milica Mijatović

On Planes Full of Immigrants

We've perfected goodbyes, made them
art to hang in long important hallways
of some diplomat's office, or in museums
where people browse, skim the notes, hands
grasped behind backs, slight intrigue on brows.
There's not much to it, though: you say goodbye,
embrace, you head to security, hiding tears
until inevitably you turn back around for one
last look. It's all in that look, that last chess
move you make in denial of the end game
that's coming. You go numb slightly here.
Somehow you find yourself at your gate having
purchased water, a soggy sandwich, and a pack
of Airwaves gum you only find here. You survey
the people around you. They're numb, too. Cheeks
red, eyes puffy, nothing much to say. You board,
flight attendants smile, you feel nauseous. Long flight
to America ahead, you catch yourself focused
on what's outside the window, what you're leaving,
and you squint until you convince yourself you see
your family squinting back, faces wet, hands waving.
You wave back and keep waving long after departure,
long after your vision has blurred. Numb still,
you doze to memories you just made, so fresh you
forget you're flying, until the pilot says you've landed,
Welcome to JFK, and only when you've stepped off
the plane do you realize the goodbye has just begun.

Garrett Hongo

Two Soliloquies from Nisei Bar & Grill, A Play in Progress

At rise we can see Blind-Boy Liliko'i, a short, thin, wiry Japanese man in his sixties, dressed in a white linen suit with an old aloha shirt that once might have been gaudy. He wears a Panama hat, very dark glasses so you cannot see his eyes, and straw sandals on his feet that might be covered in tabi socks. He holds a silver National tricone resonator guitar in his hand as he crosses the stage from right-rear to downstage center and takes up a seat on a stool placed there. He settles himself, tunes the strings, and plays a few chords, then hitting a few explosive, sliding notes before he speaks. He is our narrator. Behind him are tables and chairs, a long bar and stools, and overhead a ceiling hung with fishnets and glass floats in the style of an old Trader Vic's. On the walls are stuffed fish, a dartboard, a Sesshū-like painting of a dragon, and, behind the bar, there is a long dirty mirror, stacked glasses and various bottles of liquor in front of it. Behind Blind-Boy sit various denizens of the bar: Harry the bartender, a stout Japanese American man in his seventies; Frito Bandito, a Chicano hustler and delivery man; the Sansei Kid, twentysomething and a pop-boy version of Blind Boy; Atlas and Flash, two aloha-shirted Nisei men playing pool; Atomic Nancy, a waitress and punk rock singer in her thirties; and Sci-Fi and Kimi, who speak in the texts that follow:

Sci-Fi Dreams of His Future Contributions to Multiculturalism

Sci-Fi sits at a table in the bar. He can be Filipino, Chinese, Japanese, or South Asian. There are notebooks, loose pages of paper, a stack of comic books, an ashtray, and various, multi-colored pencils arrayed in front of him on the table. He's dressed in a green corduroy coat, red dress shirt, and lavender bell-bottom jeans. His hair is long, worn in a page-boy style. He smokes a cigarette and occasionally sips from a bottle of beer as he speaks.

(Aria parlante)

At first, I thought I'd create a Martian *kung-fu* expert—
An extra-terrestrial Bruce Lee I then decided should be Venutian.
But I bagged that story—too many technical problems.
I felt I couldn't build up the verisimilitude of actions,
Events in the story all too familiar from movies already.
And I didn't know enough about the fundamentals of *karate*
So I couldn't describe the development of his style very well.
And then the fact that Venutians are fishlike people
Slightly lower on the evolutionary scale than earthlings,
Sort of like the Creature from the Black Lagoon
Or the Beast from Twenty-thousand Fathoms
Or the Monster of Cape Piedras Blancas . . .
Well, I figured they would develop something more flowing,
Because their hands are like fins or flippers,
So I went back and tried to change it,
Figuring *tai-chi* or *aikido* was more their style,
But then nobody could attack anybody
And then I wouldn't have a story so I bagged it.
So now I'm working on one about an Asian runaway
From a maximum security ward of a futuristic prison,
A psychiatric care center, see?
I just got my Letter to the Editor printed
In the "Interplanetary Transmissions" section
Of this month's *Space Digest* and I was checking it over
To see if they've cut any of it. They'd rejected my story,
Saying it was too esoteric. I'd invented this special space language,
Sort of like an interplanetary Esperanto, combining
Tibetan syntax, Old English, aborigine tongue-clicking,
Computer beeps, and CeeBee truck driver's code
So that the various humanoid races throughout the galaxy
Could communicate in a Slanglish of their own,
Cut across cultural barriers and eliminate
Ethno-centrism by having a common language—

The old idea of language as culture.
There wouldn't be any minority groups
And hence no racial oppression, no racism, right?

Kimi Imagines Herself as a Kite

*Music from the house fades into the jukebox. It's Kan-Kan Musume and
Tokio Boogie-Woogie sounding tinny and faraway. Then 40s big band
music kicks in, "American Patrol" by the Glenn Miller Orchestra perhaps,
or else "Moonglow" from Artie Shaw. Harry is behind the bar wiping up
glasses and stowing them in pyramids in front of a long, dingy mirror. Out
in the serving area, Sci Fi is reading comics at a table, a young woman is
grading papers at another table, and Atlas and Flash are playing pool at the
far side of the room. Kimi, a Japanese American hairdresser in her fifties,
sits at the bar, playing solitaire and smoking a cigarette. Dressed plainly in
a two-piece outfit with a sweater over her shoulders and black pumps, she's
speaking to Harry.*

(Cavatina)

In my generation—in *our* generation, we cared how we looked.
You look at Atlas over there. . . .
(She gestures with her cigarette)
He's only now letting his hair grow over his ears.
It used to be he always had a haircut, always looked nice.
That's why I wanted to marry him. All the girls did!
I like men to have their hair like Atlas and Flash did—crew-cuts!
Like they been in the Marines or the 442nd.
I don't want to sound prejudiced, but, in those days,
Men were men. Nisei men were real men.
That Karen-*chan* used to have real sloppy hair—
The kind that hippies have, you know?
Long, way below her waist, hard to manage.
But I set her straight, curled it all up and gave her a Frizz.

And the older women listen to me too. I'm a trend-setter.
I know all the latest styles and colorizing.
And I know what looks good for *them* in particular.
I really know the Japanese head and facial features.
I've studied it! And I make my girls study it too.
That's why everyone trusts me, why they always come
To Kimi's Kurlers and Parisian Style Salon.
Because I care and serve an integral function in the community.
I always give respect, call the older ladies as X-*san* and not Y-*chan*.
Just a little touch that reminds them we're mature women.
We Japanese are quiet and subtle like that.
At least in our generation. We take pride.
We Japanese are a great people. A strong people.
We came over in boats to work as common laborers
And managed to do very well for ourselves, despite . . .
During the war, I came out of camp on a work-service order,
Had a job here waiting for me, working in a candy factory
Wrapping butterscotch rolls. I went to beautician's school at night
Because I was thinking about the future.
It wasn't easy for a young, single Japanese girl then.
I rented a room in Boyle Heights and slept in a bed
With two other Japanese girls I knew from camp.
One painted shower curtains. The other wrote for a Black newspaper.
Most men wanted *real* things like a job in a parts factory,
To get a car and buy clothes and help their families
Get a fresh start after the war had us all locked up.
They wanted to get in on the American Dream again.
Me too, I suppose, but all I really wanted was to get out of camp,
Go away, go find myself a place like a fairy-tale land
Where girls grew out of trees and drank water from the birds—
Where I didn't have to be just a cute Japanese girl with a bad haircut.
I used to dream I had magical powers and make the seasons change.
I'd go for long walks in my dreams all over a city with parks and monuments,
And there would be cherry blossoms, pink and white puffballs
In trees lining the streets like clouds wherever I went.

I'd pretend I'd a special spell to make all the blossoms appear.
While I was at work once, I remember wanting to be a kite,
So I could fly away and still see everything,
Still be attached to a tree on the ground by a string.
I wanted to escape but be able to come back,
Still wanted something to hold me down, I guess.
I thought that would be the perfect thing—a kite made of silk
With bamboo ribs and a string of phoenix feathers for a tail.

Sara Burge

And Then There Were Deer

It's Saturday when I hike the trail
around the lake with my husband and teenage son.
Hot for September, and the path we have followed,

snaking slowly and painfully up a hill,
finally begins to flatten. I lead
and see the deer first, nearly camouflaged

in the foliage, but not quite. She sees me too,
and then I see her fawn behind her.
I stop, begin to say something, when

behind me, my son begins a confession.
An *I need to tell you something*, a slow beginning
and my lungs feel the ache of the hill, I need

to rest a moment, I have been waiting for this,
I know what is coming.
I have no idea. And then it is here.

And I could say a million things.
I should say something meaningful and motherly.
I say, *Look. Deer.*

Roy Burkhead

MEMORANDUM: To Whom It May Concern

The desk in the front row, far
Left will remain unoccupied
For the rest of the semester.
The spot was almost empty every Tuesday and Thursday, anyway.

Over-extended and stretched, the occupant would cross
The double-yellow lines in the hallway—swerving
To miss his fellow students—and return
To his lane in time to burst through the door and plop down, late every day.

His theatre minor prepared him well
To deliver his lines:
Overslept, missed the bus, raining: simply someplace
Else.

Now, forever a freshman, he lingers:
Deejaying at the student-run radio station,
Attending the chapel on campus,
Volunteering wherever volunteering is needed.

He delivered his last
Lines not in class or on the stage,
But to a fellow traveler:
"I guess I just killed us; sorry dude."

Expressions of sympathy may be given every Tuesday and Thursday
In the form of vacant stares
At the desk in the first row, far left
Space.

Denise Duhamel

I Love My Feet

You have carried me so many miles, up and down
subway stairs, as I sprinted to my plane's gate,
on the beach, your prints becoming a part of the landscape
until the waves. You were the ones to tap the car's brakes,
the gas, press down on bicycle pedals. It's true
that for a decade or two I abused you, cramming
you into pointy toed stilettos, making you work
twice has hard just to keep me upright. When I turned
forty and made amends with flats, you forgave me,
even rewarded me as I hiked along. You carried
my oh-so-many pounds, each one three times
the pressure on your soles. You bore me in good cheer
with only the occasional twisted ankle, nary
a blister. I know we are one in the same—
yet according to an article by Stephanie Pappas
in *Scientific American*, we women tend to see
our bodies in parts rather than whole.
I have hated the flab on my arms, my big nose,
but I have never hated you. You're my body's universe
as I massage you using my reflexology chart—
my shoulder pain under your baby toe, my nervous
stomach in your arch. You helped me jump
over puddles, dashed me out of the rain. So let them say
we're vain as I pumice and lotion you, thank you
by painting your nails. There is poetry in your very pace,
heel/toe iambs as we stroll and I write these lines
in my head. You were the last part of me to slide
from my mother's body and will be the first part

to slide into my casket. I have never been barefoot
and pregnant, but I will be barefoot in death—
I'll put you up at last so you can relax.

Denise Duhamel

The Gig Economy

After two delays my plane lands
in Fort Lauderdale at 1 a.m.
I drag my suitcase to the "ride share"
platform and wait for Lucia
from Lyft to pick me up
in her dented silver Corolla. Lucia
is in law school and drives all night
while her kids are asleep
at her dad's. She's a single mom,
first generation college student,
aspirational stickers—*you've got this,
reach for the stars*—on her dash.
She's glad I'm not drunk, unlikely
to puke. We have a laugh
then I ask her what kind of law
she wants to practice. She launches
into her internship, medical malpractice,
and the paralyzed teen who was
misdiagnosed at three, given
the wrong medicine. She describes
the home videos of a cherub child
running around the yard, splashing
in a swimming pool. Then the agony
of a bedridden adolescent.
Lucia said it was hard as a mother,
watching the boy's parents suffer,
suing the pediatrician. *I hope they got
justice*, I said, realizing I sounded
naive and lame. *Oh*, Lucia said,
*I worked on the side of the doctor.
We won. It was awkward, but,
I mean, that's where the money is.*

John Minczeski

Portrait of Topazia Alliata by Renato Guttuso, 1931

Donna Ammantata, Ritratto di Topazia

Here she's a madonna before a stone arch,
A train crossing the viaduct behind her,
Smokestack billowing. A shawl drapes
Over her—an oval, like the moon
She holds closed with her left hand.
A searchlight and the infinite jest of clouds
Clotting the background. It's the future
She's looking toward, and who shouldn't be
Afraid. The past is little more than a slogan
Unless it's a political movement.
A train in the background and electric light
Brightening her face and neck. Who wouldn't
Be afraid, looking ahead as she does.
I love looking out the window at night,
Watching the shadowy selves of the interior.
A few lights across the street make
The exception that proves the rule.
I am in St. Paul, young Topazia is in Palermo.
In the hour glass of the future, each grain
Glows with its own aura. The window
Reveals little of the window itself,
The argon gas sandwiched between double panes.
Somewhere behind her is the Mediterranean
—Middle Earth. Her father's eyes failing,
She read the life of Buddha to him;
The noble eightfold path.
The future is a feather she can hold.
No bird can wear it so well.

Anna Leigh Knowles

To the Ohio River Valley

The city wakes in pairs
of crossed fingers. Steel

bridges string ellipses
          over the river's blubbering mouth,

deep as a baritone. The current turns
and golden flax shifts in its wind-shattered shell.

                    It hears me coming through

the liturgy of spring. Trains ring bottles
of milk in the refrigerator and laundry
                         drips into the flowers. Like bad teeth,

blinds lilt and lodge behind windows.
I heard it too—

this blunt life overfilled us with belief.

If that cloud-heavy dusk, its ore-laden strata strung
                    like an embroidered purse,
                    heavy with idleness

and gossip, extends an arthritic hand,
calls me home, who will sit with me? The one

who has refused truces with the wheel
                         of memory—cleave me

instead, open-mouthed, loosed
from my own story so I may drink

               the spring-fed revelation
                         of returning.

Nonfiction

Alice Gray Stites
Chief Curator, Museum Director for 21c Museum Hotels

Portraiture, Inside and Out: Alfred Conteh's *Aaron*

From the micro systems at work in the human body, to the macro—the social, cultural, economic, and political forces that shape how we see and experience self and other, the artworks featured in *Fragile Figures: Beings and Time*, a current exhibition of contemporary portraiture at 21c Museum Hotel in Louisville, Kentucky, illuminate the complexity of identity, revealing intersections between vulnerability and power in portraiture. Individual and group identity are approached through direct references to noted works from art history, connecting past events to current issues, often quoting from the canon of art history to examine the contemporary human condition. Suggesting a cyclical, rather than linear perspective on the most powerful of forces, the passage of time, these works reflect the evolution of portraiture as a platform for capturing how we construct and project our identities within the rapidly changing and precarious analog and digital worlds we inhabit.

Central to the exhibition in both form and content is Alfred Conteh's painting, *Aaron*, part of his ongoing visual exploration of how African diasporic societies are fighting social, economic, educational, and psychological conflict both internally and externally. Using acrylic paint, soil, and atomized steel, Conteh paints people in everyday environments, utilizing this unexpected combination of materials to highlight his subjects' simultaneous heroism and vulnerability. Conteh endows his subject with a regal presence; his shimmering likeness is larger-than life, yet the metallic dust highlighting his features is also corrosive, symbolizing environmental and social degradation and suffering. Conteh writes, "The honest and false narratives of history embodied in this series are primarily personified in patinated colossuses that commemorate the people, culture, and battles that the populations they tower over have fought and continue to fight. We are at war on two fronts."

Conteh began his *Two Fronts* series in 2017, explaining that, "Well when it comes to that perspective, thematically for the last few years my work has been about Black empowerment and specifically Black economic empowerment....I wanted people to see the faces of those who are marginalized. For you to look into their eyes. When it came to those portraits, I think they were very telling of the people who live here. The whole series is about people who live in Atlanta. It's not just the expression."

Aaron's furrowed brow and introspective expression convey a multifaceted interiority, wherein he is wrestling with pressures exerted from inside and out, illuminating the complexity of Conteh's subject matter: the effects of gentrification on Atlanta's Black population. Conteh's decision to examine the concurrent economic, environmental, and psychological degradation of the Black community by portraying a single character personalizes these challenges, which have been brought to bear by generations of those in power, and which continue to shape the individual identities, experiences, and perceptions of those without: the two fronts are faced, but cannot be surmounted, alone. And yet, Conteh imbues his subject with latent power by portraying him as a colossus, shimmering with metallic dust. Invoking art history in his use of scale and material, Conteh creates an image of tremendous, tremulous strength, like the ancient statue that towered over Rhodes, and one whose beauty and importance are highlighted in gold, as are the portraits of the divine and powerful that have dominated the art historical canon. By appropriating and subverting these conventions, Alfred Conteh offers a transformative vision of the genre, demonstrating that contemporary portraiture can reveal the fullness of our shared humanity.

On the cover
Alfred Conteh, *Aaron*, 2018
Acrylic, atomized steel dust, and soil on canvas
Courtesy of the Collection of Laura Lee Brown and Steve Wilson,
21c Museum Hotels.

Fiction

Whitney Collins

The Apartment

When the oldest sister returned from the nursing home to bid the apartment a final farewell, a traffic jam greeted her at the complex's entrance. On either side of the arching brick gate—flanked by sturdy, tangerine marigolds, and ripe, cattle-made mulch—sat a honking bottleneck of residents, some trying to enter, some trying to exit. Complicating the congestion was a fleet of police cars, a fire chief's truck, an ungainly hook-and-ladder, two ambulances emitting a low whine, and a local news crew in an Action 26 van. Most everyone, including the oldest sister, had emerged from their cars to get a better look at the holdup and see what the cause might be, but when nothing of obvious delay presented itself, the oldest put her hands on her hips and left her two younger sisters and their five, grown children in the minivan on the side of the road to march into the thick of things to inquire. This was the sort of thing the family expected of the oldest because she expected it of herself.

"We'd just left the Arby's across the street when we saw the commotion," said a fresh-faced reporter to the oldest.

"What went down at the Arby's?" the oldest asked. "Lunch or a story?"

"A story," the reporter said. "A lady found a battered diamond ring in her order of curly fries."

"Battered?" said the oldest, craning her neck and lifting her skirt and stepping into the marigolds. "As in beat-up? Or as in dipped in egg wash and flour and sometimes buttermilk?"

"Oh, funny," the reporter smiled. "I didn't think about battered as in beat-up. I meant battered as in fried."

The oldest pressed on. She liked to get complete stories. She liked to be the first to hold something before presenting it to others, like some sort of midwife. It was what she lived for. She was the one who'd researched their father's medicines and told the doctors a thing or two about interactions and grapefruit juice. She was the one who'd solved their mother's vein problem with compression socks imported from

Estonia. She was the one who'd suggested the middle sister wear the blue dress on the blind date, and now, see here? Thirty years of marriage. The oldest was always listening, always eavesdropping, always doing the self-less thing. She'd find out what the traffic jam was all about, just as soon as she found out if the lady left the Arby's with the ring.

"Did she keep it?" she asked.

"Yep," the reporter said. "It was at least two carats."

"I bet she was thrilled," the oldest said, hands once again on her hips.

"Not really. She thought her boyfriend was proposing." The reporter laughed. "They're still in the parking lot fighting." The reporter motioned over his shoulder to the shopping center—the same shopping center that had lured the three sisters' father (and eventually mother) to the apartment complex forty years ago.

The oldest turned and squinted—she loved to witness a good public squabble—but all she could see was an ocean of rubberneckers. She stomped her foot once, like a draft horse banishing flies, and the bitter perfume of crushed marigolds filled the air.

"They've built this center," the father said to the mother, who stood at the kitchen sink in their two-story brick and washed nectarines. "It's designed to look like an English village, and it has a grocery store, a dry cleaners, a First Security bank with a drive-thru, a Hallmark shop, and a service station. There's even going to be one of those brand-new Arby's."

The mother lined up the clean nectarines audience-like on a tea towel and said nothing; she knew the father was heading somewhere stubborn.

"And just across the street from this center that has *everything* you need—I mean everything your heart could ever desire—they've gone and zoned the Stratton farm for apartments."

The thought of living in an apartment made the mother think of mannequins in a storefront, of the motionless, live lobsters that turned beige with complacency in the supermarket tank. But still, she got in the car with the father to see what all the fuss was about. They drove out of the neighborhood and past the elementary school. Past the hardware store and dress shop and ice cream parlor. Past the florist and diner and

Episcopal church and out to where the countryside could be seen in the distance, a green ocean lapping.

When the nearly completed Tudor Shoppes appeared on their right, the father and mother crossed the road and took a left through the Stratton farm entrance. The tall brick arch had once heralded the beginning of a Thoroughbred farm but now announced fields of fresh pin oak stumps and hundreds of wooden stakes tied with bright pink ribbons. It looked like a cemetery for little girls. The father drove to a particular set of wooden stakes, the Buick bouncing in the grass like a dinghy caught in the wake, then he put the car in park, climbed from it, and sighed.

"This one right here," the father gestured. The mother tottered from the sedan in her white patent leather pumps. "It's a four-plex. Two apartments up, two down. We'd be the one on the lower right."

He meandered around the wooden stakes that conjured nothing domestic to the mother. She walked through a patch of clover that would someday be her bathtub.

"See, if we're downstairs, we have patio access." He waved his hands at the sky, a salesman. "We can sit right out here on our porch furniture and eat beef stew off my army plates and look at this sky. This whole big sky. It'll be like moving to Montana."

The father had always wanted to go to Montana. The mother looked about. There was a four-foot-tall milk thistle in the middle of it all.

"What goes there?" she asked.

"A new Amana refrigerator," the father said. "Avocado green."

The mother brightened a little. "What about my roses?" she asked.

"You will have your roses," the father promised. "Times two."

One week later, the father and mother rented the invisible apartment before a shovel even thought of turning the earth. In the following ten months, the meadows of pink-ribboned stakes gave way to a sea of brick-and-aluminum four-plexes, broken up here and there by stripes of new, white sidewalks, and grass seed cloaked with straw, and indefatigable maple saplings. The father and mother were the very first tenants to move in. For three weeks, their car sat by its lonesome in the fresh, black parking lot like a skull in the desert. The father made good on his promise and planted twenty rose bushes in the empty back yard.

The mother washed various fruits in her new sink and arranged them in various ways on the new countertop. The father and mother wore white socks to protect the unworn carpet. They puzzled over the modern faucets and hollow-core doors and tried to decide if they minded that the conditioned air smelled like carbon paper. Most of their days, however, were spent on the apartment's selling point—the patio—looking at the sky and eating off army plates, like two pioneers who'd made a wrong turn in the gold rush.

At the time, the three sisters worried that their father and mother had made a terrible decision. That they'd sold the family home way too early—they were just fifty and fifty-three, for Pete's sake—to live in a real estate debacle. The sisters lamented to one another the lack of shade trees and birdsongs and friendly passers-by. They detested the continuous knocking of distant hammers and the relentless sunlight. They especially hated the sky, that monotonous cell wall of a sky that made Montana seem like a death sentence. They thought the whole scenario looked like something from a bad western movie set. The oldest took to calling it "Rawhide" under her breath.

"Where're the tumbleweeds?" the oldest wanted to know. "If they had a cat, a hawk would've snatched it by now in that desolate yard of theirs. No chance of getting a dog now. Plus, the sun will fry the new grass. Forget cookouts in that heat. Are their curtains lined? They'll never sleep past six. Their upholstery will fade. Wrinkles. Skin cancer."

The middle was more concerned about the height of their furniture. About how it didn't suit the apartment and how the china cabinet scraped the low ceilings. "I can't stop thinking about their armoire," she said. "I stay awake at night thinking about the armoire. That apartment was not designed for an armoire."

The third said the least, but when she did, she always made the most practical points. "Of all the lots, why the one on a hill? They have to walk up eighteen steps to get to the front door. That will spell trouble as they age." At this the sisters went quiet for the hundredth time thinking of groceries and sleet and hospital bills.

*

Sometimes the sisters went out to lunch at the ice cream parlor in their former, childhood neighborhood. They ordered the things they had always ordered—olive nut sandwiches on rye toast and pellet-iced Cokes and peach pie with a scoop of butter pecan—*just one slice; we'll share*—before putting on sunglasses and parking across the street from the old family house and going through an entire box of tissues. The new owners had yet to plant geraniums in the window boxes, and this offered up a thin sliver of hope that everyone was miserable and that maybe they'd move out and their parents could move back in.

But just as soon as the sisters fretted ten pounds each off their hips, their mother's new blush roses bloomed, and the maple saplings opened up like a thousand green umbrellas and automobiles filled the Stratton Place parking lots like shined red, black, and silver shoes lined up by stoops. Neighbors began milling about the once-farm, whistling and terrier-walking and getting to know who was who and why they'd moved. By the time a Baskin-Robbins went in at the Tudor Shoppes a few months later, the father and mother were settled and content. The sisters were reluctant to admit that the apartment was growing on them. Somewhat.

But the oldest sister knew *somewhat* wasn't good enough. *Somewhat* was like a loose thread that needed to be snipped. If she didn't push the sisters past *somewhat*, all they'd see for the rest of their lives was a bright red string on a black wool coat. The oldest could not tolerate ambiguity. She knew a stand had to be taken for the sake of the family.

"Like it or not, we must now view the apartment as a sibling," she said. "A baby sister that we should dress and encourage and dote upon."

The middle sister and third sister agreed as they always did when the oldest proposed something, partly because she was always right, partly because they wanted her silent. That very day, the three sisters went out and bought the baby striped pink-and-brown wallpaper for the hall bathroom and a new, wood-paneled television set for the tiny den and a brass wall hanging of seagulls in flight to go above the sofa.

*

The idea that the apartment was a sibling gained momentum. Whenever the sisters came to say hello to their parents, they brought something for the fourth sister under the guise of it being a gift for their father or mother—a ceramic soap dish, a tiny crystal clock shaped like a wheelbarrow, a bathmat, a fern, a paperweight, a wastebasket. On their visits, the sisters also brainstormed ways to arrange the things their parents had collected over the years They tucked photo albums in the entryway closet and tackle boxes under the guest bed. They stored winter coats in suitcases and put the suitcases behind doors. Finding a place for every belonging of the father and the mother was like solving a crossword. There were five rooms now instead of ten, but the oldest insisted that eliminating items was out of the question. *Mother might not use the sewing machine anymore but look how much our new sister likes it tucked into this sunny corner of hers. Look how happy we are making her!*

Soon, the baby sister was giant and plump, crammed with sentimental stuffing, a living museum the three sisters flocked to on the weekends and after work. They ate olive nut sandwiches off tin plates and leaned against her smudged patio door. They slept in her tiny guest room when their husbands were away on business, safe in what felt like the crook of her elbow. The oldest particularly fussed over her, fluffing up her velvet drapes, running the cordless sweeper over her shag, folding her pink towels and stacking them in the closet like layered strawberry cakes.

In time the three sisters had five children among them, and they brought them to the fourth sister, where the children hid and sought among her suitcases. Under beds, her cold steel tackle boxes calmed their thumping hearts while they waited to hear *Come out, come out, wherever you are!* The children meandered all over the fourth sister, like ants on a dozing picnicker. They opened her drawers and poked at the grandfather's pipe tobacco. They stole handfuls of pastel butter mints. They found box turtles under the fourth sister's viburnums and painted their names on the turtles' backs with the grandmother's fuchsia nail polish. Sometimes, the husbands came for crowded family dinners, their scalps flush with her popcorn ceiling, their long limbs folded underneath the tiny dining table, and the fourth sister cramped their style.

The oldest smiled at what she had engineered. She might as well have been the one who'd hammered the pink-ribboned stakes into the earth from the get-go. She was like Magellan, Ponce de Leon, Columbus. An irrepressible explorer who had not just seen the possibilities, but also had the good sense to insist on a contract. The Pilgrims didn't start a new chapter by just wandering around the New World admiring the corn. Someone, likely an oldest, had insisted on the Mayflower Compact to get everyone past *somewhat*.

Before long, the fourth sister was herself a woman—wiser than all of them. Her backyard grew dark green with shade, her roses were switched out for introverted begonias, her maroon shutters were painted Dutch blue by the Stratton Place management in Phase II. The best and last sister eventually settled into the earth from all the activity and demands and sacrifice. She sagged in a distinguished way—a spray of orange lichens grew about her chimney, a corona of moss topped her shingles. Years somehow passed as easily as a flock of brisk, spring cumulus, and a time came when the three sisters couldn't remember their father and mother living anywhere else. Sometimes, the trio drove past the old brick two-story where they'd spent their entire childhoods, and they politely smiled in the same way they did to bygone classmates at reunions. *Well, they seem nice*, they'd muse. *I wonder how we never crossed paths.*

The oldest knew: all they had ever really known was the apartment. All they had ever loved was her. The oldest smiled. She had recognized the family's queen and groomed her for the throne. What if she'd never seen the fourth sister's potential? The apartment would have been a failure, that's what. Their parents would have had to have found a third place. If the oldest hadn't paid attention, the family would have been broken apart. Thanks to her, everyone was still together and happy. She deserved some credit for that, so she took some.

*

By the time the fresh-faced reporter had relayed the entire Arby's story, the oldest was joined by her two sisters and their five grown children.

"What's going on?" the middle sister asked.

"Yes, please," said one of the children. "Tell us: did somebody die?"

The oldest didn't show how maddened she was. She'd never *not* gotten the scoop first.

"I've been trying to figure it out since I left you. No one knows anything. Not a soul. Not even this young man."

The oldest had been fanning herself with her checkbook, which she now used to point at the reporter as if he owed her money. The reporter turned away and pressed his earpiece firmly into his ear.

"What?" the family heard him say. "That's impossible." The reporter lowered his voice. "You have to be kidding me. I have to see this for myself."

Then, without further acknowledgement, as if the family were made of vapor, the reporter let go of his ear and waved to a cameraman and bolted toward the entrance.

"Well, that's it," said the oldest, putting her checkbook back into her purse and snapping it shut. "I'm going in."

"Me too," said several of the children in unison, as if they were still school-aged, eating cake from the grandfather's tin army plates and not already bothered with majors and minors and first mortgages.

The family knew Stratton Place well—its fencerows and tree lines and walking paths—and they deduced, without having to waste time on discussion, that they could outsmart the entire rubbernecking throng by winding their way back to the minivan and then up a small hill to the complex's jogging trail. This trail meandered through a brief, fabricated forest of white pines and after an eighth of a mile, if the family wasn't stopped by authorities, they could veer off and be deposited adjacent to the old four-plex. From there, they'd have a better view of the entrance and whatever it was that was going on, and if it turned out to be nothing of real interest—say a false alarm over a homicide—then they could get on with what it was they came to do in the first place: bid the apartment a final farewell.

So, the three sisters and the five grown children traipsed in the noon-day heat back to the minivan. They stripped themselves of their cardigans and jackets, which they wrapped around the women's purses and hid in the rear of the vehicle, before climbing up the short embankment from the roadside and disappearing into the white pines, led by the oldest.

Aren't we clever? their gait seemed to say, as they marched in a determined, related line of bobbing auburn heads and steely eyes and clenched jaws. *Who knows Stratton Farm better than we? Our family's been here since the tulip poplars were the size of yardsticks. We remember when Baskin-Robbins still served Black Walnut, when this whole development was nothing more than a field of fluttering pink ribbons that terrified crows. If you want to know how to outsmart the masses here at Stratton,* their posture (especially the oldest's) announced, *well, just watch how we work.*

The family skipped along the abbreviated leg of trail, grateful for the scent of pine sap and angles of cool shade, but when the trail spit them out, what the family saw—or rather didn't see—crumpled their short-lived territorial pride. The former four-plex was now a three-plex. There was still the lower left apartment and the upper left apartment and the upper right apartment, but where the adored fourth sister had once sat on the lower right, settled and entrenched in the earth like a weathered matriarch curled on her side, was now nothing more than a gap. A blank rectangle of air, a missing tooth, through which the sisters and cousins could see straight through to the backyard. Where five, bulging rooms had at one time housed pink towels and *Reader's Digests* and tin army plates and polyester suits (and recently nothing at all in the name of assisted living), there was now simply ether. It was as if a single toy building block had been poked through with a careful finger and slid away from a child's stack without consequence.

The family could see where yellow police tape was tied around the handrails of the eighteen steps and then wrapped around the front yard trees and what they could see of the backyard trees. Inside the taped area, there was a sheriff and a fire chief and a woman in a hardhat and a man in a suit. They were gesturing toward the space, presumably wondering how the upper right apartment had not yet collapsed and how to prevent it from doing so.

In the parking lot, a crowd marveled at the spectacle. The residents of Stratton Place had never witnessed such excitement and terror and novelty inside their well-maintained and predictable little complex. The sisters and cousins stood under the pines in a steely auburn line and held hands, as if frozen in a game of Red Rover.

"Do you think it was a bomb?" one child whispered.

"Was it a fire we missed?" the middle sister wondered aloud.

But as they stared, they could see no signs of smoke, no demolition, no lingering debris. Not one corner of drywall, not the bottom half of the exterior downspout, not one beam of lumber or fluff of pink insulation remained to indicate the apartment had ever existed. The beloved fourth sister, quite plainly, had vanished.

"She's gone," the oldest murmured, ashen.

"Who is?" asked a cousin.

"*It*," said the third sister. "She meant *it's* gone."

When their father first fell bringing the groceries up the eighteen steps, the sisters offered to do the weekly shopping in shifts. When the mother broke her ankle two months later on her way to church, the middle and third became discouraged until the oldest stepped in and made a schedule of who would drive the mother to and from the Wednesday prayer service and on what week. When both the father and the mother became too feeble and foggy to water the begonias or operate the washing machine or manage a can opener, the oldest insisted on finding a way to divvy up caregiving duties, despite everyone—husbands, children, physicians, the middle and the third—suggesting a change might be in order.

"Of course not," insisted the oldest. "We can manage."

So, for a time, the three daughters went about shuttling and spoon-feeding and sponge-bathing until it became clear to the middle and third that the father and mother could no longer function, neither in the apartment nor without full-time care. At an impasse, the three sisters met at the old ice cream parlor over three slices of peach pie. The middle and third were ready to negotiate, but the oldest was unmoving. She knew it was not her parents' independence she was clinging to. It was the fourth sister, *her favorite sister*, the last and the best. The one she, the family midwife, had delivered and held up for all to see.

"I don't see why one of our children can't rent the apartment," the oldest said. "Or why we couldn't hire a full-time nurse."

The middle tried to be diplomatic. "I'm not sure the children want to live there, but that's a good suggestion."

"We could rent it out while Mother and Father recuperate somewhere," the oldest said.

"That's a thought," said the middle.

"Or we could…"

"What?" the third interrupted. She cut the tip of her pie with her fork and then pushed it aside. "We could what? We don't own the apartment. We can't rent it out. And recuperating? They're not going to get better."

The middle coughed. The oldest stared. The third always had been the voice of reason and this time she was willing to be punished for it.

"We have to face facts. The children don't want to live there. We cannot afford both a full-time nurse and the apartment. It's time for a new chapter. It's time for them to move." The third sister looked at the oldest and said the obvious thing that everyone, save for the oldest, had wanted to say for quite some time. "Come on. It's just an apartment."

The oldest turned stony at this. Cold and looming. An iceberg. "Did you say *just an apartment?*" She set down her fork and placed both palms on the table to brace herself. "Well, fuck you, Serena. And fuck you, too, Jeannine. I'm the one who introduced our sister to both of you in the first place. Neither of you would have even known her if it weren't for me. You would have never seen her as a person if I hadn't stepped in. You would have only seen her as property. A prop."

There was a moment of shocked silence before the middle sister began to quietly weep and the third sister motioned to the waitress for her check. The oldest continued to grip the table. "It's not over, you know."

Nothing more was uttered after that, and the three sisters paid separately. They walked wordlessly to the car they'd come in and drove back to the apartment where the third daughter told the father and the mother that they'd be moving. By the end of the week, the middle sister found a full-service nursing home. A week after that, as if it were her idea all

along, the oldest gathered her two sisters and the five grown children
to help in the packing. They divided the bath towels and linens and
Reader's Digest condensed books eight ways. They bartered fine china
for tackle boxes, crystal champagne flutes for vinyl records. Tea sets and
encyclopedia sets were broken up because everyone wanted a piece. One
child got the sugar bowl, another three saucers, another A-J of the Bri-
tannica, another K-T. The brass wall hanging of seagulls in flight was
deemed the most coveted piece, so they drew straws for that, as well
as the tiny crystal wheelbarrow clock that everyone had always secretly
admired and the vintage Samsonite suitcases that evoked both simpler
times and trips untaken.

The packing and divvying started off well enough, with trips down memory lane and prudence taken with bubble wrap, but by day four of the
apartment's dissection, the sisters grew overwhelmed. There were forty
years of Tupperware lids and forty years of school pictures and forty years
of recipes and coupons and newspaper clippings. The five rooms expanded
and extended and excreted until the fourth sister was a beached whale of
artifacts. The further the sisters tunneled in, the more complex the fourth
sister grew. They'd never known how much she'd stored and hidden, how
much effort it would require to empty her of herself. They felt betrayed
and ashamed. They bickered and cried and apologized and stormed out
of rooms and pussyfooted back in. With the fourth sister splayed open,
it was clear how lost they were. With the fourth sister splayed open, the
oldest made the decision to never let her go. She made the secret decision
to sell her car and rent the fourth sister with the money. She'd take up
riding a bicycle. She'd come to the sister during the day when everyone
else was at work or school and she'd lay on her stained carpet and smell
the ghosts of butter mints, hear the distant scrape of forks on army plates.
She would have her all to herself. It was what she was going to do.

On the eleventh day, the apartment finally lay barren and cold like a
gutted fish. All that remained inside of her were nail holes and bright

squares on the dull paint where pictures had hung and the lingering scent of pipe tobacco. Outside, the three sisters gathered to dig up the begonias, splitting the tubers and placing them into trash bags to place dormant in their respective basements.

"Who got the army plates?" the oldest asked.

"Michael did," said the third sister.

When they were done, they carried the trash bags through the patio doors and noticed, but did not mention, how vacant the apartment seemed, like the blank gaze of the newly deceased. Then they proceeded out the front door, and the oldest locked it with a single silver key, before descending the eighteen stairs. She did not make a fuss or cry, because she knew they were coming back. After they'd all gone to the nursing home with the children to see if their father and mother had been hooked up properly to the things that kept them alive, they would return for a final goodbye. There was no reason to pretend like it was the end when it wasn't. Especially for the oldest.

The family stood under the pines for at least an hour. From a distance they watched three local news crews mill about and set up cameras and gesture and shrug. They could see the reporters point, they could see their mouths move, and even though they could not hear them, they knew they were calling the fate of the apartment "a mystery," "an enigma," "a phenomenon unlike any other." The three sisters knew the disappearance of the best and the last would be the talk of the town. Over dinner that night, families would turn on their televisions and stare at the day's top story while their potatoes grew cold. People would talk about it for generations to come.

Past the police tape and up the eighteen steps, the woman in the hardhat had been joined by several others in hardhats. Momentarily, a Stratton Place maintenance official appeared on the scene, driving a small excavator. He maneuvered beneath the upper right apartment and extended its bucket to one of the unsupported corners, a temporary solution to a problem that was apparently not a problem at all.

"Should we go?" one of the children finally asked.

"Sounds good to me," said another.

The three sisters had nothing to say. They followed their children back the way they had come, through the angles of cool shade and the scent of pine sap. And at the end of the glum parade, everyone piled into the minivan, save for the oldest. She held back, by the last of the fragrant evergreens, bereft inside. She reached into her right pants pocket for the cold comfort of the apartment's silver key but found there was no key to be felt. With a little flutter of panic, the oldest patted her rear pockets, the chest pockets of her blouse. She slid her fingertips into her left pants pocket, but still: no key. Her flutter of panic dropped as quickly as it had risen, a moth's sudden death. What did it matter? So, there was no key; there was also no apartment.

The oldest descended the hill and climbed back into the driver's seat of the minivan. She wasn't hungry but everyone else was, and they ended up at the Arby's across the street. The middle sister and third sister and the five grown children ordered elaborate sandwiches with packets of sauce, large milkshakes and hot turnovers and curly fries. They overtook the restaurant, clumped like begonias, and their voices were loud, like forks on army plates. How quickly and easily they seemed to forget or accept that the apartment was now missing.

The oldest went off to a corner alone with an order of small fires. She sat in a band of sunlight and wondered: where had her fourth and favorite sister gone? Perhaps she was now a boxcar, a big rattling rectangle that had decided to go see the world, filled full with things that made people happy—crates of nectarines and pink towels and little crystal wheelbarrows. Or perhaps she had decided to live a simple, utilitarian life. Maybe she was now a mailbox. Maybe she had flown out from under the four-plex on a gust of wind and out to where the countryside opened up and the sky was once again a monotonous Montana blue. Maybe she had shrunk down to something she had always wanted to be: small and unremarkable—a little metal box, perched on a lonely fencepost, her only requirement to hold postcards and water bills and long-awaited love letters.

The oldest, dazed, ate slowly. Maybe the apartment's fate was worse. Maybe she'd died from a greedy sort of love. Forty years ago, the three oldest sisters had first despised the apartment, then resisted her, then patronized her with doodads and fluff and lace. They had made demands of her. They had used her to feel safe, to cramp their husbands' style, to entertain their children, to justify trifles, to strip the father and mother of their dignity, to never grow up. Maybe, in the end, they had only run her down and dismantled her, like wolves might an elk, rendering her nothing more than a carcass, a hull. Maybe, the apartment was no boxcar or mailbox. Maybe she was just a servant who had been waiting patiently, for four decades, to know the freedom of being useless. She had served and served and at her first opportunity, the fourth and favorite and final sister had simply gotten up and walked away.

The oldest sat in the corner considering this, mindlessly chewing, until she bit into metal. She concealed a gasp, darted her eyes left and right, then reached up to her parted lips and produced a silver key, battered. Her eyes darted left-right a second time. She wiped the batter from the key and admired it. When she was done, she slid it into her right pants pocket, and when the middle sister and the third sister and the five grown children weren't looking, the oldest got up from her table and began walking. She went right out the door of the Arby's and through the parking lot of the Tudor Shoppes. She marched right past the entrance of Stratton Place, past the fragrant manure-mulch and marigolds, and down the road that eventually led to the countryside, to the fields dotted with cows and horses and little mirror ponds. It was a disappearing act of sorts. And it was the sort of thing that no one expected of the oldest because she didn't expect it of herself.

Glen Pourciau

STEM

Haven't heard a sound upstairs all morning so I go up to check on Dave. Usually, I hear his footsteps shuffling to and fro overhead.

I find him curled on the floor, his back to me. He's conscious and I try to get him to talk.

"Are you hurt?"

"Not hurt, just down. I'm staying. I know what I'm doing."

"You can't stay there."

"I can. Don't try to make me talk."

"Why don't you lie in bed?"

"If I lie in bed, I'm doing something."

"You're lying on the floor. What's the difference?"

"On the floor, I'm doing nothing."

"I can't disagree with you."

"I'm talking too much."

"And that's doing something?"

"Leave me alone."

I retreat down the stairs.

A few weeks ago, he took a seat in the backyard and stared at the grass. I couldn't get him to move. After four hours I tried to pull him up, but he resisted. I got our next-door neighbor, Milton, to assist me. We leaned over and talked quietly to him. He finally rose, waving us away, stumbling until his legs steadied beneath him.

I can't leave him by himself in the house. Our daughter comes on Saturdays so I can go to lunch with one of my girlfriends.

I can't sleep upstairs with him anymore. He keeps getting up during the night, looking through things and taking things apart. One night he woke me up and asked who I was and how I got inside his house.

*

I mount the stairs hours later. He's in the same position. I put an empty bowl, his meds, and a bottle of water in front of him.

"May I help you with anything?"

He doesn't answer and he won't look at me.

"I'll bring you food."

"Don't," he says.

"Will you talk to me?"

"When I move and do things, that's when my troubles start. And when I speak. All of my troubles come from me, so the best thing is to say and do nothing."

"I hope I don't make you feel that way."

"It's nothing to do with anyone but me. Can we please stop talking?"

"Let me know if I can help you."

"No one can."

In the morning I make him a plate of eggs, buttered toast, and bacon. I imagine he smells it coming toward him.

I set the plate on the floor. He closes his eyes to shut it out.

"Do you want coffee?"

"Don't bring anything. Encouragement disturbs me."

He's had a few sips from the water bottle, just enough to wet his mouth.

"Please go away and take the food."

"I'll leave it in case you change your mind."

"I'm trying not to be rude."

"Why don't you at least roll over?"

"I'd rather not look down the stairway. It puts ideas in my head."

"You think about going down?"

"Please accept what I'm doing."

"That's hard to do."

"I'm asking."

I start away.

"Take the food," he says.

I pick up the plate.

                                          *

I sit on the back porch and talk to myself. Should I call someone? What should I do? Is he wrong to shut himself down? Can he sustain it?

Not a sound out of him all day. I don't go up. He has asked me to accept him.

At dawn, his groans wake me up. I wonder if he's in physical pain. I've heard him groan at his thoughts before, creating noise to drown them out. I hear him talking as if someone is yelling at him, maybe someone in a nightmare.

I climb the stairs. He stirs.

"Are you my brainstem?" he asks. "Why are you disturbing me?"

"Let me help you."

"How? Are you supernatural?"

I go to the bowl, take it to the bathroom, and dump it. I put it back where it was.

"If you don't get up, I'm calling Milton. We're going to pick you up and carry you downstairs."

"What do you think will happen then? Is the floor less comfortable there? Will you kick me until I do what you want?"

"I'm not going to kick you."

"You'd like to kick me, wouldn't you? You've got your life to lead and I'm an obstacle. I'm an obstacle to myself. Even my own body doesn't want me to lie down until I'm not here any longer. My brainstem won't leave me alone, and I can't make it stop."

"I don't know what to do."

"You can't do anything, and you can't accept me. I'm unacceptable."

Dave gradually stretches his curled body out, cursing himself. He puts an elbow under him and sits up. He covers his face, groaning into his hands. I take a step toward him as he gets on his feet.

"I failed," he whispers.

Verena Tay

Bibliophile

So new, so enticing . . . On the shelf, the book lies—sleek, lean lines, unblemished cover, virgin pages, the text promising fulfilment for mind and soul. How can she not succumb to such charms?

Behind her, her husband asks, "Is it really necessary?"

"Yes."

"I don't think so."

"Are you my mother?"

"Sometimes."

In exasperation, she elbow-jabs his chest. How to make this man she loves understand her ever-present hunger? As a child, she adored reading, though books were a luxury. Dad was always sick, and the family had to make do on Mum's earnings as a cleaner. Weekly visits to the public library barely satisfied her appetite. While she spent hours absorbing grimy dog-eared paperbacks and pen-marked non-fiction, she always dreamed she would one day hold pristine texts within her hands for her eyes only.

"Really, honey," he continues, "so what if nowadays you can damn well afford to buy any new book that you want? Must you get everything that grabs your attention?"

Her shoulders slump over. He is right. There are too many books in their condo stacked high everywhere, a veritable buffet of all new, mostly unread titles—a far cry from the famine of her youth. Perhaps she should buy time instead to read now leisure is a premium with work and all. She resists. He smiles. Then on reaching home, she regrets.

Brookes Washington

I Remember You

God don't like ugly. My mama always told me that when I played in the sun too long. Afterwards, her eyes was black crystals searching me for errors that was too dark. Her face was always sure, so when she spoke, no one knew if she was telling the truth or not. That made her almost always right. She looked almost white, and her hair was so fine she didn't need a perm to straighten it back into place. She wore red everything cause can't nobody tell you nothing when you wearing red things that make you look like Old Hollywood, sparkly and unreachable. From afar, she was almost a white woman; up close, she was passing.

The older I got, my desire to wear more red things grew. Of course, I was a little darker than mama, but my hair was fine. A little too thick, too black. But I wanted worship and learned not to make things look too thick. So, the hot comb cemented my curls to my scalp every night. I stayed out of the sun and forgot about heavenly things. My mama had crystals for eyes that found flaws, but I prayed for rubies that could remove the parts of someone that didn't fit my image. I never valued God's unwanted things until I met Ralph.

His skin reminded me of the color blue. It was two shades darker than a tree's bark. Man could make a river smile. His hands were made for work and wanting. And when I looked at Ralph, I saw how shiny and glistening I was to him, better than a popsicle in the heat. I loved the idea of his love for me. He slept most of the marriage with love and trust like good men do. But our hands never met in public places that mattered.

"Don't bring no nappy-headed babies here," my mama sang in my ears when my belly had become fat with a mixture of me and Ralph. Mama wouldn't belong if her children didn't. My first born, Jean, reminded her of my daddy, a high yellow man from New Orleans who always smiled like he had nothing to lose. Jean was the world's reminder he was shades removed from white ships and black cargo, putting the world at ease for their sins. Ain't nothing like forgiveness, and Jean was exoneration. But Lucille, my second child, was all Ralph and all my shame.

She came out tiny, midnight fists balled, ready to fight. I held her as my mama held me, and I cried because she was my unwanted thing. Her skin was a different version of heaven that blocked my private room decision to fade into a white crowd and never have the want to find myself again. There was nothing red or shiny or passing about her. There was no room in me for her.

One night, Lucille disappeared, and Ralph never looked at me again.

Renato Barucco

Cherry Tree

It started with the cherry tree, the summer the kid turned ten. The last day of school coincided with the dreadful trip to the farm with Mother. They joined Father out there, past the pine forest, far from the village. Far from Elio, his only friend. They called the place El Dos for the shape of the main pasture, a hump surrounded by shrubs.

There was nothing to do in El Dos but follow Father's orders in the hayfields on sunny days or come up with solitary games when it rained and, for that reason, wish for rain. Being stuck out there with aging parents was no fun. The kid had no one to play with except Nero, Luna, and the cherry tree.

Nero was an old dog. He followed the kid around out of obligation, always looking for something else in the distance—a rabbit, another dog, Father, who had Nero's absolute loyalty. A faint whistle from Father was all it took for the dog to dump the kid without hesitation.

On the other hand, Luna was devoted. She was the kid's shadow out in the hayfields. If the kid ran, she ran. If the kid jumped, she jumped, against all odds. When the kid rested, Luna rested. Sometimes, he'd lie on top of her. Her round belly went up and down in synch with her slow breathing, a special lullaby. Luna smelled like the good parts of summer. But unfortunately, friendships with cows were doomed, and the kid knew as much. Sooner or later, likely in the winter, Luna would end up on a plate. Father and Mother were religious and ate the body of Christ every Sunday with gusto. The kid didn't want to eat anyone he'd known. Better keep some distance and accept Luna for what she was—a summer fling.

The cherry tree became the kid's best friend. In its constant search for sunlight, it leaned on one side, like the Tower of Pisa, overlooking a modest pasture cut in half by a slim waterway. The tree's trunk was thick and gentle, covered in green spots. The branches extended upward, easy to climb, heavy with leaves. Aluminum tins hung from them as a way to scare off the birds. From the tree, the countryside looked different, manageable. The kid used to play games from up there. Eagle, in which the kid acted as if he were an eagle governing his kingdom from the skies. Buzzard, a dramatic reversal, in which the kid was on the look-out for real buzzards with one objective—scaring them away when they circled above the farm's chicks. And flying horses, in which the kid tied strings around the necks of his toy horses and made them swing from the branches like a curious breed of wingless creatures.

But his favorite pastime was cherry picking. The kid loved cherries. Cherries made the days tolerable. It had been that way for as long as he could remember, which wasn't long. He'd eat so many of them at once his belly hurt. (And when that happened, he couldn't tell Mother, or else he'd get an earful.) His fingernails were purplish for days after the harvest. The cherry tree was an easy friend. From its branches, the summers were sweeter.

But things changed that year. It took a glance to realize something was wrong with the tree. The trunk was dark and dry, the branches bare, all pale leaves, not a cherry in sight, a terrifying sight. The trees in the neighboring farms seemed to be doing just fine. The kid waited a few days for a storm, hoping for a miracle, but when the rain did come, the tree remained the same. Lifeless, sterile. He then asked Father about the cherries.

"The birds ate them."

Birds. What birds? Why only now? What about the aluminum tins? It made no sense. But Father didn't like to argue, so the kid swallowed his questions and spent that summer cultivating the unbalanced friend-ship with Nero and the doomed one with Luna. He still climbed the tree, which only made losing the friend he once knew more real. The branches creaked, and the leaves fell. From up there, the air smelled like something had been burning, and the clouds were darker. There was a subtle, opaque haze on the crest of the hills. It was a sad, long summer.

The cold months were worse, marked by loss. The butcher bought three-quarters of Luna. The remaining quarter ended up in the freezer and eventually made its way to the dinner table. In the fall, Hare hunters shot Nero because his barking scared away their prey, or at least that was how Father explained it, not a word more. He didn't seem sad about it, but the kid noticed a lump going up and down in his throat the way it happens when people cry. Selfless until the end, the cherry tree ended up into the wood stove, burning so fast it was gone in three days, the coldest of winter.

The following summer, the kid was prepared. With no friends left in El Dos, he brought new ones with him, books he'd borrowed from the library, novels that weren't right for his age. Mother and Father were too busy to care. The stories of Edgar Allen Poe and Angela Carter. *Frankenstein. Dracula. Strange Case of Dr. Jekyll and Mr. Hyde.* Thrills and frights took him to places with blurred boundaries between the real and the imagined, a comfortable dimension in which the difference between thoughts and dreams was ambiguous. Sometimes, the kid forgot if something had indeed happened or if he had read about it. Had there been a storm? Had he heard a cry coming from the woods? He read the books sitting on the black stomp of the cherry tree, glancing at his surroundings every other page or so. The cherry trees from the other farms no longer bore fruits, but the branches of the small trees at the sides of the path leading to the barn were still heavy with sour cherries, which he didn't like at all, except in the winter, after they'd spent months in jars with alcohol and sugar. He wasn't supposed to have those, but again, no one noticed.

Some of the pines in the forest were dry all the way to the roots, bright orange in the sun, something that kid had never seen. He shook his head. The birds were blameless. Something in the soil was hurting the trees.

As a teen, the boy gained access to more books. With the bit of money he saved working on Saturday afternoons in a local workshop, he bought paperback copies of recent novels, scarier stories. Stephen King's boys and their childhoods full of shadows. Anne Rice's languid vampires. Thomas Harris's lambs. He still spent his summers in El Dos. He had to. Season after season, he took note of the changes. Wild berries and hazelnuts disappeared from the underwood. Figs rotted on the branches. On the vines, grapes grew smaller, drier. Father acknowledged the changes. That was how nature worked.

"Not every harvest can be good," he said. Grunts and wheezes did little to conceal the lack of conviction in his voice. A palpable veil of dread covered the land, feasting on life from within. The boy wondered if maybe it was all his fault. Had he lost the ability to tell apart reality from fiction? Were his beloved stories of terror contaminating his perceptions?

The boy took on drawing the following school year. Charcoal at first, oil paints later. He honed his skills with the help of a local artist who took note of his rare talent and took him under his wing. The kid learned to portray living things, from fruits to human bodies, trying to emulate the art he loved. Da Vinci. Caravaggio. Rembrandt. Shadows again. A lot of darkness and minimal light. Chiaroscuro gave his work a tenebrous quality.

Art accompanied the boy through another season in El Dos, where death was now everywhere, undeniable. Frogs floated in the pond, belly-up, bloated and yellow. All the rabbits died in their cages in a matter of days. There were fewer and fewer butterflies flapping around during the day and no fireflies at night. Carolina, the stronger cow in the barn, gave birth to an emaciated calf the color of ash, which did not survive. Out of excuses, Father remained silent. He couldn't stomach the truth, so he sold the livestock and gave up on farming as if that sacrifice would purify the air of whatever was killing animals and plants.

In the fall, a doctor from the city visited the province. From behind their curtains, villagers looked as she collected bags of soil, filled vials with water from the creeks, and walked around the countryside holding suspicious gadgets. Two months later, she toured the town councils of the province and presented her findings. There were alarming levels of pollutants in the air and on the ground, contaminating the pastures, the rivers, the springs. Poison had been falling from the sky for years. She believed the foundries at the bottom of the valley had been melting toxic metal scrap for decades.

But the townsfolk ignored the alarm bell. After all, it was the word of an outsider—a scientist, a woman—against what they knew, and what they knew was that the foundries gave work to men, and men had families to feed. It didn't help that the pollution wasn't the sort of intruder villagers could see with their eyes and shoot with their rifles. Invisible, it scared no one.

Like everyone else, the boy heard the rumors and remembered his cherry tree. There came the realization that his inexplicable attraction to darkness and shadows didn't cloud his senses. The opposite. The macabre stories of his novels and the dark paint on his brushes had helped him withstand what surrounded him, the real horror humans unleashed on the land. An older teenager now, he reminded his parents of the cherry tree and the dry grapes and the rotting figs and the rabbits and the fire-flies. Still, Father responded with a stern silence, and Mother turned her back, returning to the kitchen sink. They prohibited him from bringing up the subject ever again.

Denial and omertà didn't stop the poison from contaminating the land. Unperturbed, lethal dust settled on the grass and the leaves, and dirty rain infiltrated the aquifers. The venom eventually reached the people, hiding in the creases and folds of their organs.

The foundry workers were the first to go, devoured by mutations in their bodies. Then the teachers at the school down the street from the factories. Elio developed cancer in his balls, and he was only nineteen. The venom spared no one, and in a matter of years, death was every-where.

The boy was a young man when his parents passed away. Mother first, with a tumor in her uterus the size of a melon. Father, a few months later, on New Year's Eve. He choked on bits of his own lungs and coughed up a single word. *Sorry.* The young man didn't shed a tear. He'd learned to confront loss with silence. He no longer painted and barely read books. He'd found new ways to cope—pain pills on an empty stomach, washed down with a drink or five.

After Father's funeral, the young man drove to a bar at the bottom of the valley for his daily fix. It was January, and the night was humid and warm even in the countryside. He sat at the bar and ordered two glasses of bourbon at once, one to down with the first pill, one to stare at, a liquid mirror. A group of men gathered around a pinball machine. Two loud fellows shared work stories. They said their employers had paid them a month-worth of wages to melt containers of metal scraps from the east. The job had to be done at night, on Christmas Eve. They said the smoke was as dark as the sky, the smell unbearable.

"Nothing good came out of the chimney," said one of the men, smiling. The color of his teeth matched the pilsner in his hand. It had been a solid gig. No one wondered why the pay had been that good, how much more the boss had profited from the job, or if money was worth what would lie ahead for them and their children, their gardens, and their pets.

The young man returned home earlier than planned. The house still smelled of chrysanthemums even if he'd already brought the bouquets in the courtyard. He sat in front of the television with another drink and another pill. His head throbbed. That night, the pain had a different texture, the bitterness on his tongue a peculiar intensity. Hopelessness. His soul ached, and pills and booze could do nothing about it.

He went to the attic and grabbed the dusty basket with the paints and brushes he hadn't touched in months and months. He closed his eyes and gathered memories of El Dos, which soon appeared on the canvas with the farm, the surrounding hills, the vines, the pastures. The colors were dark. But shadows exalted the light, and far in the distance, splashes of red animated the branches of a tree. Cherries.

Mary Popham

At Delaney's

Uneven rows of cars lined the parking lot at Delaney's Tavern. As Kara Fields sidled past them, kicking up gravel with her high heeled pumps, she looked for her friend Marci's silver Honda. She spied it parked by the dumpster near the back door. Kara side-stepped rainbow-colored oil puddles and passed a car whose recently quieted engine released its heat with a tick-tick-tick.

She pulled at the brass-studded door marked "Employees Only" and was thrust into cold darkness. Her senses adjusted from the lit parking lot and a silent October breeze, filtered through the trees of nearby Cherokee Park, into a blast of cigarette smoke and the music of a live band. Smoking habits had long been ingrained in many of Delaney's patrons who were over thirty, (thus the club's nickname "The Wrinkle Room"), and Kara wondered how Delaney's would change if management adopted smoke-free rules. In Kentucky, drinking and smoking went together.

As for the music, Kara, almost forty, reflected that the later generations kept remaking songs from the previous decades. It seemed they were trying to recapture what looked like the innocence of pre-Nine Eleven.

Bright lights over the bandstand and behind the bar outlined square tables centered with small candles. Kara whiffed the familiar malty sweet-sour smell of beer as she maneuvered a path through the outside tables and along the edge of the dancers. It was Friday and her night off which meant Marci had to work. On Saturdays they switched waitress duties.

Kara chose Friday as her free time at the nightclub because they served Happy Hour two-for-one drinks; the crowd came in early and stayed late. Women customers were most likely looking to find a dinner-and-movie date for Saturday, while the men wanted to pick up somebody for the night. If successful, the women wouldn't be coming to Delaney's on Saturday. Kara figured that covered the agenda for probably 99% of the women and 1% of the men. Which added up to a lot of disappointment for most of the people in the club.

The bandleader, Andrew McCleve of the Louisville Night Experiment, began the keyboard introduction to "I Left My Heart in San Francisco." Kara figured that the young, yet balding soldier stationed at Fort Knox had walked in, all smiles and back-slapping. The band played songs for special friends as a way to let the crowd know when someone popular, like the west coast PFC, had arrived. Special friends earned a tribute from Andrew's band, particularly the ones who bought drinks for them during breaks between sets.

From all the time she'd worked at Delaney's, she'd never had them play her favorite song. In fact, she mused, what would "her" song be? Some old mournful blues by Etta James, like "A Sunday Kind of Love," or Billie Holiday's "The Very Thought of You," letting their moods match how she felt after yet another break-up.

"Over here," sang out Marci. With a nod of her head, she indicated a table on the edge of the dance floor. One of her arms encircled a tray of beer bottles and mixed drinks. With her free hand she grabbed the "Reserved" sign and Kara sat down. She frowned at the volume of the music at this close range. She thought they were playing louder than usual to be heard over the din of customers who shouted to show what a good time they were having.

"Jack and Water?" asked Marci. Kara smiled at her, nodded, and glanced at the stag line in front of the bar. Some swiveled on bar stools and drank beer while gazing at the TV, muted as the band played a set. Several craned their necks back and forth to see the dancers through a steady stream of women who paraded along the pathway. Some of her friends called this aisle "the meat rack," stopping as they found someone they knew. The squealing and kissing got the men's attention and also let everyone know who was there.

Kara didn't want to see Corky Thomas. Since he'd been dating someone new, they were probably home doing what she and he used to do. That is, they weren't out looking for somebody to stay home with.

"He's here," said Marci as she lay a paper napkin on the table and placed the Jack and Water on it. The napkin's picture of a cocktail glass with bubbling champagne and stir sticks soaked up the moisture.

"By himself?"

"The bitch is with him."

"Oh God. I ought to get out of here."

"You'll do no such thing! This is *your* place, not his."

Kara took the first sip of her drink, always the best one. Sometimes she felt a twinge of disloyalty because she chose it over her native state's Kentucky bourbon, but she liked the distinctive charcoal-mellowness of Jack Daniels. She thought her fellow Kentuckians at Delaney's would forgive her since it was the most popular whiskey they offered. She drew the line with anyone who polluted it with Cola, which is what Corky used to do.

The first week after they broke up, she had stayed home and let the TV wash over her. The second week, she made plans for every night after work till bedtime. She pondered her sadness over losing her love and found that it wasn't how lovable Corky had been. It was simply added to her other failures to find the man she would spend her life with. She added this discouragement to the long list of her single life of unsuccessful attempts to find love.

As far as romantic advice, she depended on Marci. Having a built-in buddy-system with another waitress helped her feel she was making good date choices. It seemed to her that in her sensitive and emotional state, her mind filled with insanity just when she needed to use all of her common sense. However, if she'd ignored Marci's advice a year ago, she could have saved herself this pain. She should have known better the first time Corky ordered Jack and Coke.

Since they both had experience in serving tables of male customers, Kara and Marci took turns alerting each other as to who was respectful to the staff, who was a good tipper, and who drank too much. She had trusted Marci's recommendation from the year before. "Look at the gorgeous guy dancing down front." The gleam from Corky's belt buckle sparkled up and down like starlight moving through the dancers.

Kara was attracted to his moves and his looks, especially his muscular shoulders and black curls. He was short and trim and danced with such enthusiasm his white shirt was damp under the arms.

Marci had often told her that when a man got a look at Kara's long brown hair and detached expression he made a beeline to ask her to dance. As a young woman, she'd read *The Rules*, the self-help book with "Time-tested secrets for capturing the heart of Mr. Right." She'd been convinced that the female authors were correct. Men want to do the pursuing. She also listened to Marci who told her, "Don't let them know you care. Men like a challenge." But that night, she made up her mind that if Corky didn't ask her to dance, she would approach him.

She remembered their first meeting. His beautiful smooth face, always smiling, drew people to him. His little-boy sweetness and Southern manners kept them. He talked a lot, but he also knew how to listen. Maybe their relationship ended because she'd broken a most important rule: she had pursued him.

Kara had broken The Rules when the band played the opening notes from the Carpenter's song. "Why do birds fall down from the sky, every time you walk by?"

"They're playing our song," she'd said to Corky as he gulped his drink while trying to regain his breath from the exertion of dancing.

He took her hand and led her to a dark corner of the dance floor. Kara hummed, "Just like me, they long to be close to you."

They dated for ten months. Kara introduced him to her friends, they went to house parties and wedding showers and family reunions, but he mostly wanted to dance. And not just with her. On New Year's Eve, he flirted with so many of her girlfriends that at midnight she'd hidden in the stairwell when the count-down began just to see if he would look for her to get the special kiss at midnight. He *did* find her and couldn't understand why she softly cried.

A country-rock song presaged their break-up: "Heartache Tonight."

She knew she'd have to end it when Marci began to see Corky in Delaney's alone after telling Kara he was working late.

"You want to date other girls, don't you?" Kara asked.

He looked startled at the frank question, but after a minute he murmured, "Yes."

Breaking up shouldn't be so hard, she thought. But the routine of every day and night got shattered. Corky wouldn't be calling in the afternoon to say when he would pick her up, or where they would meet. She'd buy no more blue tops because he liked the way they brought out the color of her eyes. She'd have to abandon Twix cookie/candies because they reminded her too much of his favorite treat. On Saturday nights, she'd watch videos with the girls or stay home alone to read romance novels while life outside her apartment went on without her. This was a world for couples.

The band began the plaintive opening of the Eagles' song: "Somebody's gonna hurt someone; Before the night is through; Somebody's gonna come undone; There's nothin' we can do."

Marci put a basket of pretzels on her table. She nudged Kara and said, "Here comes that bottle blonde. She's headed this way."

Kara looked up to see a woman, in heels that made her taller than Corky, pulling him by the hand. Her skirt showed muscular legs and her top dipped way down in front to show the fullness of her breasts. They threaded their way through the other bodies whose arms and legs punched the air, stopping at the bit of platform exactly in front of Kara's table.

As Corky and the blonde began to dance, Marci bent to Kara's ear. "I can't believe she's got the brass to drag him over here to show him off in front of you, like a prize!"

Kara took a deep breath. She glanced around to see men turning their heads to stare at the blonde woman's body, while her own friends looked at her own face for a reaction. She obliged by tilting her head up to Marci and laughed as if she'd heard the funniest comment ever made. She couldn't believe that Corky was aware of what his new girlfriend was doing: putting her stamp on him in front of her.

"That floozy got what she wanted. Didn't you know she flirted with him every chance she got?" asked Marci.

Before Kara could answer, the woman in front of her began to flail her arms, but she wasn't dancing. Her high heels had slipped from under her, and she fell completely to the floor, her legs splayed out. Other dancers moved out of the way, while still watching the accident. Corky pulled his date to her feet. She hobbled and he shuffled with her back across the dance floor.

Kara's delight came in little spurts. She felt sweet, soul-soothing revenge flood her sore heart. In the back of her mind, she knew she was angry with Corky, but it felt good to see the woman who tried to hurt her get thrown down by her own feet. Perfect that it was right in front of Kara.

The band continued with the song. Kara picked up all the individual sounds of the keyboard, bowed electric guitar, the drums, and fretting bass. A man smelling of Brute cologne bent and asked her to dance. Friends greeted her with smiles as she took the stranger's hand and made her way to the dance floor.

J. D. Strunk

Tokyo, 2031

The boy is young—six, maybe seven. He sits with his parents on the roof of their concrete apartment building, nothing separating their damp heads from the stars but empty space. The humid air is thick enough to chew. Many families surround them. Everyone knows each other. No one talks.

Just yesterday the boy had been excited: People were talking about the approaching storm, and he liked storms, despite the anxiety they gave him. He liked to watch them from the window of their sixth-story apartment. He liked to see the lightning splay into kinetic fingers over the bay, and to feel the thunder shake the apartment walls, any sense of danger tempered by a deeper feeling of structural safety.

But this storm had not been fun. It had lasted too long, and it was *loud*. And now, with the storm having finally passed, and with evening fast approaching and the building's backup generators having failed, the residents sit in familial circles on the roof, waiting to be rescued by one of the dozens of helicopters blinking red on the horizon.

The boy is miserable, but not because of the storm. His misery is rooted in the fact that there is no dog sitting beside him. He feels this entire experience would be but an inconvenience if only there was a dog beside him. In particular, a golden Shiba Inu named Haruki. It has been over 24 hours since Haruki escaped his collar and ran away from the boy's father. "He sensed the storm," his father had told him after, as if this explanation made the loss somehow bearable. And now the boy watches the sun setting on the water-logged city, fearful that he will never see his dog again.

Ten stories below, dozens of boats float down the city streets—now canals—navigating between the concrete apartment buildings. Most of the boats are small: kayaks, sailboats, single engine fishing boats—boats slight enough to have been sheltered inside. The boy has been watching the boats pass by their apartment building for hours. The water beneath them is brown and smells of sewage. The air is acrid and lingers in the back of the throat.

The boy leans far over the ledge of the roof. His father sees and tells him to be careful. The boy hears the request but makes no reply. He is scanning the water for Haruki. Some of the boats contain dogs, but there are no dogs visible in the water, neither swimming nor floating. The boy's hope is setting with the evening sun when he sees a grouping of small specks in the distance. One of the larger specks is bobbing up and down in the water. The speck moves in and out of the long shadows cast by apartment buildings. From this distance the boy cannot tell if it is Haruki. Indeed, he cannot tell if it is a dog —it could be a microwave, or a tire. But it is this very uncertainty which gives the boy hope.

The boy turns to his father, tells him what he sees. The father joins the boy at the edge of the building. He follows the boy's arm and squints out at the water. "That is not Haruki," he tells his son. "Just part of a tree, caught in a current."

The boy loves his father, but in this instance, he does not believe him. His father is pretending it is not Haruki in order keep the boy from do-ing something rash. Which is smart, as the boy is about to do something rash.

For several minutes, the boy watches Haruki drift in the distance. The dog is coming no nearer to their apartment building, and at his cur-rent speed, he will drift out of sight by sundown. If the boy seeks to save the animal, he must act now.

The boy looks to where his parents sit, some meters away. They are talking, quietly but intensely. The boy knows he needs to wait until they are no longer looking in his direction. The boy does not like deceiving them, but this may be the only chance he has to rescue Haruki. And so, when his parents are distracted by a distant explosion, he moves quickly across the roof of the building, past the families huddled on blankets, and toward the door that leads to the stairwell. The boy runs down nine flights of stairs, until his progress is impeded by stagnant water in the stairwell. He backtracks to the landing of the second floor. The windows on the landing are old, but they are not locked, and he is able to push one open. He sticks his head out of the window and finds black water a meter below. He sees no way of escape and feels his hope shriveling into nothingness when the dark outline of a wooden rowboat drifts into view. The boat is small, and contains only one person—an old man with a long white beard. The man is wrapped in clothes so dirty and disheveled as to be indistinguishable from rags. He is propelling his craft with a single oar, alternating sides with each row.

Just as the boat passes in front of the boy's building, the man looks up, as if called—the boy remains silent—and spots the boy where his small head protrudes from the window. The man slows his boat by dragging the face of the oar through the water.

"Hello there," says the old man.

"Hello," says the boy.

"What a strange place to be. Where is your family? Safe, I hope."

"My parents are on the roof."

"And why are you not on the roof as well?" asks the man, placing a hand on the concrete wall to steady his craft against a current that wishes to carry him away.

"I saw Haruki in the distance. I need to rescue him."

"Who is Haruki?"

"My dog."

"I see," says the old man, stroking his beard sagely with his free hand. "I bet Haruki will know to come home, if you just give him some time to sort out his thoughts. In the meantime, you best return to the roof and be with your family."

The boy shakes his head vehemently. "Haruki is the best dog in the world. I cannot leave him."

"Hmm," says the man. "And where did you last see Haruki?"

"He's not far." The boy points past the man and into the near distance. "He's just over there."

The old man follows the boy's finger and looks behind him. He looks back to the boy. "My eyes are not what they once were. Soon the sun will set, and it will be dangerous to be out on the water. If I promise to go and look for Haruki, will you promise to return to the roof?"

The boy considers the old man's offer. "If you take me in your boat," says the boy, "we can rescue Haruki together."

The man opens his mouth as if to argue with the boy, but no admonishment comes out. Instead, his eyes scan the horizon, where the red sun is fattening behind a misty sheen of phosphorescent clouds. Perhaps thinking of his own stubborn children or grandchildren, the old man agrees to the boy's terms. He moves the boat directly against the building. With great care, the old man stands, thereby helping the boy drop safely into the boat. The craft sways ominously for an unnerving few seconds before leveling out. The boy sits down, facing the old man.

"You must guide me in the proper direction," says the man, putting the oar into the water.

The boy turns around inside the boat; he sits in the bow, facing the open water. A quick scan of the horizon reveals a row of recognizable buildings. The boy points. "I saw him there, between the green building and the red one."

The old man takes in the buildings in question, then nods. He begins to paddle, alternating sides like before, but now with greater urgency. The man's muscles strain as the boat begins to pick up speed. Cords in the man's neck grow taught as he paddles faster and faster. The boy turns around to look at the man, shocked by the sudden burst of speed. He had assumed the man's age indicated frailty, but this man is anything but enfeebled—the waters part easily before his modest ship, and what had seemed from afar to be a great distance is soon traversed.

As the boat drifts into the gap between the buildings, the old man stops rowing. The small craft cuts smoothly through the water. As the boat slows, the boy's eyes dart to and fro, desperate to find his Haruki's head bobbing amongst the flotsam. The water is littered with hundreds of objects, from socks to sofas, and a proper inventory takes several minutes. At its conclusion, the boy's head drops: No dogs.

The boy begins shaking, first with anger, and then with grief. The old man does not intervene—only begins rowing again. It is many minutes before the boy looks up. When he does, it is to notice that the boat is back in front of his apartment building.

"It is time to go home," says the man.

"The roof is not my home," says the boy.

"Of course not," says the old man. "I am speaking of your parents."

The boy's brow furrows, but he makes no argument. The man creates a foothold with his interlocked fingers, and the boy places a waterlogged shoe into the seam. With masterful agility, the old man steadies the boat as the boy's weight is returned to the building. Once safely inside, the boy turns around and looks down on the man, who is growing dimmer by the second with the advent of evening.

"Where will you go tonight?" the boy asks.

"I too am looking for someone very dear to me. I will keep searching."

"All night?"

"And into tomorrow."

"Be careful," says the boy.

"You as well."

The boy runs up the stairwell, two steps at a time. At the final landing before the roof, he sticks his head out of the window. He means to thank the old man, but the boat is already gone.

As he opens the door to the roof, the boy can hear his father calling his name—the boy has never heard his father's voice so loud. When the father spots the boy, he continues to yell the boy's name, though the tenor of his voice changes: What was previously panic is now equal parts anger and relief. But by the time the father reaches the boy, the anger is gone, and only relief remains. The father picks up his son and holds him tightly to his chest. The boy tells his father that he cannot breathe, but the father does not release the boy. The father lifts the boy as though he were a baby and carries him across the roof, to the corner where his mother sits alone. At the sight of the boy, the mother jumps up. She hugs the child, still in his father's arms.

It is many minutes before the boy is permitted to leave his parent's embrace. And it is only with a stern warning from his father that he is permitted to walk back to the edge of the building.

The boy looks out onto the water, but it is now too dark to see anything save for a scattering of candlelight in the windows of the neighboring buildings. The boy abandons the view and heads back to his parents. He sits between them, nestling his head into his father's chest, his legs dangling across his mother's lap. The boy is suddenly exhausted and will soon be asleep.

"I miss Haruki," says the boy.

"I know," says his father. "So do I."

Soon the boy's chest is rising and falling with regularity. The father looks to his wife, whose features are barely visible. Despite the darkness, he sees her smile as she puts a hand on the boy's forehead. She gathers a blanket around her and closes her eyes.

And now the father's eyelids grow heavy.

And now all are asleep.

Cornerstone

poetry by writers K-12

John Gabriel Sperl

On the Subject of Fairy Tales

Pigs fly and fairies lie under the sun,
all peaceful, at ease, steeped in each minute.
But not all is grand, for when they're finished,
they pack up and go, into dark they run.

For modern thoughts, like greedy hunting dogs,
are lapping up these childish little tales
and tying them up on to rusty rails,
left behind to rot like forgotten logs.

But all is not lost, inquisitive tot.
Your folks are writing up your secret wish
of lil' fairies and flying flopping fish,
and making smiles upon the human lot.

O, forgotten tales may decay and rot,
but we foster them like the freshest crop.

John Gabriel Sperl

Blossoms Shudder

Blossoms shudder
in anticipated wonder,
and the pollination train goes by.
Pollen encountered,
flowers powdered,
all the way back to the hive.
Drones hover
while the queen lays another
generation to keep us alive.

Rihaan Phillip Kapoor

Indifference Kills

for Pincus Kolender, holocaust survivor

It's a wall that blocks my suffering
A shield that blocks my pain
Nothing is something
That's easiest to maintain

At first, you loved me, or so I thought
Now you leave me, here to rot
Beaten, stabbed, robbed, and gassed
Do something, there's nothing more that I could ask
You could have won but you didn't act
Now I suffer, day by day
From something which you could have saved

Even if I live, I know in my head
Because of you, I am already dead

Indifference kills
Indifference kills
Indifference kills

Thousands watch, as they rip my hair
Take my clothes, strip me bare
But in their faces, they have no care
We just lost our humanity

Indifference kills
Indifference kills
Indifference kills

But look up, onto the sky
There exist a bright shining light
Brave souls, willing to fight
Unlike you, they do not hide
So bright, so strong, all can see
Because of them, I am free

Seth Niemann

No More Drama

Red lips moving, but no sound.

Once exploding with words,
has now fallen victim to silence.

The curtains rising and with it,
our esteem falls ever so low.

Are we silent with fear?
Or worse, with sorrow.

Memories of how it felt flood back,
And with them, the tears.

Hold it in because no one cares.
We pull our chins up to make it unnoticeable.

Not one hand to help you up.
Only stares.

Matilda Reinhart

Untitled

Lying in my bed
I can't get it out of my head
Arms are like jello, I feel so weak
Its like im on a mountain peak
It cannot go around
I must get down
I start to fly, I start to dream
I scream
Why is life such a wondrous thing

Jenny Zhu

The Fragile Heart Runs on Venom

you know you've hit rock bottom when
you laugh at your own jokes to fill the silence,
direct melodramatic confrontations in the stage of your mind,
or realize that your tears, which had once carved hollows into your cheeks,
have long been shaken away, lost
in the steady current of time
but don't you remember
how you were so angry that your voice shriveled in your throat?
and felt so miserable that instead of crying,
you laughed at your reflection in the mirror, because
there was nothing more pathetic than seeing
the product of your naïveté, your
blind hope, and how desperately you had clung,
delirious, to your lovestruck daydreams

because if i painted every lie i've ever told myself
on the canvas of my body, they'd
cover every inch of skin, ravel
in every strand of hair, blacken
my heart as they pulse through every vessel, and
still pour from my eyes, spurt
from my mouth, leak
through every crevice;
crimson waterfalls so thick that the red has melded into black
and i choke back tears of obsidian ink
of starless skies, and
strangle myself with my words
i sit, choking
on my delusions, peering
at the world through a gossamer veil, woven

with the starlight from those nights i laid awake,
suspended between hope and tears, clinging
to that smile he'd flashed my way, whispering
a secret that only our minds can unravel

and my heart hurts;
no—
it doesn't hurt;
it aches, it burns, it's been rubbed raw;
chafed by my ribs every time i steal glances from across the room,
unrequited
and i want to cry, scream
for this love story i had ripped apart, for
this beautiful dimpled boy i'd broken into pieces and tossed away
to be put back together by someone else
but this time, i would stay
i'd hold you
until the skin eroded from my fingers, until
my soul was bleached away, until
i faded to nothing more than a shadow,
vacant, unseeing eyes still
transfixed upon your face
and even then,
my mangled heart shriveled, moth-eaten;
i'll still be there, and
i'll still be yours:
two ghosts in the night

Amity Doyle

Noted My Day

Rolled out of bed before my alarm
Forgot to wait
Saw the fragrant flowers tied up all in a vase
Began to walk slowly
Then quickly ran to thee
Because I had just realized, realized that I was free

Emma Catherine Hoff

The Cloisters

How many hands were before?
How many people deconstructed,
then reconstructed?
What people made it so
this powerful building
towered over the sidewalks
of Manhattan and not England?
Who sat Jesus on his donkey
in the middle of the floor
despite signs saying not to touch?
Next time, I will tap the floorboards.
Maybe the artists
will be underneath
with the monks.
In the unicorn room,
the beast thrashes
on the walls, on each and every tapestry.
You can never be free
until you walk out the door
and still you see the inhuman
faces of the figures standing there
with their weapons and dogs.
Still you see the fangs
that sink into flesh.
Howling figures hang from the ceiling.
You are afraid to sit down,
you don't want a corpse to fall on you.
Another room is filled with candles
and golden busts.
Who separated these heads

from their bodies?
Virgin Mary holds her child,
paint peeling off his limbs
as you count the many ribs
that go from his shoulder
to his waist.
He is a tiny man with a beard.
Even the walls
are a thousand years old.
Does it make you feel small?
How many hands are now?

Contributors' Notes

Merle L. Bachman, the granddaughter of Yiddish-speaking immigrants who came to New York around 1912, grew up in Albany, NY. A poet who delights in writing prose and exploring the arbitrary boundaries between genres, Bachman has published a scholarly monograph, two poetry chapbooks, two full-length poetry books, and an anthology (with co-editor Anthony Rudolf of London) featuring selected poems of the Scottish-Jewish poet A. C. Jacobs. Her translation of selections of Rosa Nevadovska's Yiddish poetry is forthcoming in 2023, and her latest book, the hybrid-genre *Thank You for Being: A Poet's Memoir of Home*, was published just last year.

Renato Barucco (he/él/lui) is a writer and psychologist based in Brooklyn, NY. His fiction has appeared in *Longleaf Review, Fiction International, Not One of Us*, and many other literary magazines. His nonfiction has appeared in *The Daily Beast, The Huff Post*, and *The New York Times*. He has recently completed a novel. More information at www.renatobarucco.com.

Marin Bodakov was born on April 28th, 1971 in Veliko Tarnovo. He holds a degree in Bulgarian philology from St. Kliment Ohridski University in Sofia. He teaches at St. Kliment Ohridski University, and since 2000, he has managed the literary department of *Kultura* newspaper. He and his wife, translator Zornitsa Hristova founded Tochitsa—an independent press for children's educational literature. Marin is the author of five books of poetry, most recently *Naïve Art* (2011), for which he received the Ivan Nikolov National Literary Award.

Kevin Boyle has published poems in *The Louisville Review* as well as other major journals, including *The Greensboro Review, Hollins Critic, North American Review, Pleiades, Poetry East, Prairie Schooner*, and *Virginia Quarterly Review*. His most recent book, *Astir* (Jacar Press), was a finalist for the 2016 Brockman Campbell Prize (judge, Barbara Hamby) and his first collection, *A Home for Wayward Girls*, won the New Issues Poetry Prize, judged by Rodney Jones. Kevin grew up in Philadelphia and now lives in North Carolina.

Christopher Buckley is editor of *Naming the Lost: The Fresno Poets—Interviews & Essays*, Stephen F. Austin State Univ. Press, 2021. His most recent book of poetry is *One Sky to the Next*, winner of the Longleaf Press Book Prize, 2023.

Sara Burge is the author of *Apocalypse Ranch*, and her poetry has appeared in or is forthcoming from *Virginia Quarterly Review, Willow Springs, Prairie Schooner, The American Journal of Poetry, Pacifica Literary Review, River Styx*, and elsewhere.

Roy Burkhead holds a Master of Fine Arts degree and a Post-master's Certificate in Writing Enrichment, both from the Naslund-Mann Graduate School of Writing at Spalding University. In 2021, he was nominated for the Paul Engle Prize for his work with The Writer's Loft low-residency certificate program (now known as MTSU Write) and the literary journal *2nd & Church*. A Kentucky native and longtime Nashvillian, he has been an adjunct English professor at Western Kentucky University (WKU), in Bowling Green, Kentucky since 2008. For the past three decades, Roy has worked as a writer and editor in the technology industry and higher education. www.rlburkhead.com/

Whitney Collins is the author of *Big Bad*, which won the Mary McCarthy Prize, a Gold Medal IPPY, and a Bronze Medal INDIES. Her second collection, *Ricky & Other Love Stories* is forthcoming June 2024. Whitney is the recipient of a Pushcart Prize, a Pushcart Special Mention, the American Short(er) Fiction Prize, and the ProForma Prize. In 2022, she received a Distinguished Story nod from The Best American Short Stories and was included in *The Best Small Fictions*. She received her MFA from the Naslund-Mann Graduate School of Writing.

Totem: America, **Debra Kang Dean**'s third full-length collection of poetry, was shortlisted for the Indiana Authors Award in Poetry in 2020. In addition to her books of poetry, she has published two prize-winning chapbooks and with Russ Kesler a chapbook of renku. Recent publications include a review of *The Lost Etheridge: Uncollected Poems*, edited by Norman Minnick, and poems in *They Rise Like a Wave: An Anthology of Asian American Women Poets, The World I Leave You: Asian American Poets on Faith and Spirit*, and *Chiburu: Anthology of Hawai'i Okinawan Literature*. She is on the poetry faculty at Spalding University's Naslund-Mann Graduate School of Writing.

A former contributor to *The Louisville Review*, **Denise Duhamel**'s most recent books of poetry are *Second Story* (Pittsburgh, 2021 and *Scald* (2017). *Blowout* (2013) was a finalist for the National Book Critics Circle Award. A recipient of fellowships from the Guggenheim Foundation and the National Endowment for the Arts, she is a distinguished university professor in the MFA program at Florida International University in Miami.

Alice Bingham Gorman's essays, short stories, and poems have been published in *The Louisville Review, Vogue, Oprah Magazine, Salon.com, The Dead Mule School of Southern Literature*, and others. Her first novel, *Valeria Vose*, an IPPY award winner for southern fiction, was published in 2018. Originally from Memphis, Tennessee, she lives in Maine and Florida.

Lennie Hay is a 2019 MFA graduate of Spalding University. She grew up in the Midwest between two cultures—Chinese immigrants and German Ukrainian farmers. A former educator, she lived in Louisville for nearly 50 years and now lives on the water in Southern Indiana and in Florida drawing energy from visual art, her family's history, and music. Her work has been published in various journals such as *Round Table Literary Journal, Heartland Review, Shanghai Literary Review, Literary Accents* and others, as well as in an anthology, *Boom.* Her debut poetry collection, *Lost in America,* is forthcoming from Broadstone Books in 2024.

Poet, memoirist, and editor **Garrett Hongo** was born in Volcano, Hawai'i, in 1951 to Japanese American parents. He grew up in Hawai'i and Los Angeles and earned his BA from Pomona College and his MFA from the University of California-Irvine. His collections of poetry include *Yellow Light* (1982), *The River of Heaven* (1988), which received the Lamont Poetry Prize and was nominated for a Pulitzer, *Coral Road: Poems* (2011), and *The Mirror Diary* (2017).

Amy Foos Kapoor is the managing editor of *The Louisville Review* as well as a multimedia producer and an aspiring children's writer. She earned her MFA from Spalding University's Sena Jeter Naslund-Karen Mann School of Writing.

Peter Kent has published poems in *Cimarron Review, Greensboro Review, Lullwater Review, New Millennium Writings, The Opiate, Smartish Pace* and other journals. His work has received a high commendation in the Gregory O'Donoghue International Poetry Competition and was a finalist for the Erskine J. Poetry Prize. These poems are from a manuscript titled "Welcome Hymn"; poems from this collection have been published in *The Greensboro Review, Smartish Pace,* and *Ponder Review.*

Rolly Kent's last appearance in *TLR* was Spring 2022; his new book, *Phone Ringing in a Dark House,* will be published later this year by Carnegie Mellon University Press. He lives in Los Angeles.

Anna Leigh Knowles is the author of *Conditions of The Wounded*, finalist for the 2021 Brittingham and Felix Pollack Poetry Prize, published in the Wisconsin Poetry Series. Her work appears in *Blackbird, The Missouri Review Online, Tin House* and others. She has received honors from the Illinois Arts Council Agency and the W.B. Yeats Society of New York. She holds an MFA from Southern Illinois University-Carbondale. For more information, please visit annaleighknowles.com.

Mary Makofske's latest books are *The Gambler's Daughter* (Orchard Street Press, 2022), *World Enough, and Time* (Kelsay, 2017), and *Traction* (Ashland, 2011), winner of the

Richard Snyder Prize. Her poems have appeared previously in *The Louisville Review* and in *Poetry East, Southern Poetry Review, Valparaiso Poetry Review,* and *Talking River Review* and in 19 anthologies. www.marymakofske.com

Milica Mijatović is a Serb poet and translator. Born in Brčko, Bosnia and Hercegovina, she relocated to the United States where she earned a BA in Creative Writing and English Literature from Capital University. She received her MFA in Creative Writing from Boston University and is a recipient of a Robert Pinsky Global Fellowship in Poetry. Her chapbook *War Food* won the Fool for Poetry International Chapbook Competition and will be published in May 2023 by Southword Editions in Cork, Ireland. Her poetry appears or is forthcoming in *Rattle, Salamander, Plume, The Louisville Review, Collateral, Santa Clara Review, Poet Lore*, and elsewhere. Her poems have been nominated for the Pushcart Prize, and she serves as Assistant Poetry Editor for *Consequence.*

John Minczeski, author of *A Letter to Serafin* and other collections, has published in *Cider Press Review, Bear Review, Rhino, Harvard Review, The New Yorker* and other magazines and journals. He has traveled Minnesota as an itinerant poet in the schools, has taught at colleges around the Twin Cities, and in various community programs.

Elizabeth Pope is a poet and painter from the Appalachian mountains of Southeastern Kentucky where she was born and raised in an Appalachian culture and a coal-culture. Currently, she lives in Louisville, with her daughters, where she is pursuing a PhD. in Humanities at the University of Louisville. She holds an M.F.A. in Creative Writing from Bluegrass Writers Studio, and an M.A. in English Literature from Eastern Kentucky University. Her honors include an Emerging Artist Award from the Kentucky Arts Council, two Pushcart Prize nominations, an Artist Enrichment Grant from the Kentucky Foundation for Women, and The 2022 Annette Allen Poetry Prize, judged by 2011-2012 Kentucky Poet Laureate Maureen Morehead. Her poetry appears in *North Dakota Quarterly, Euphony Journal, Red Rock Review, Appalachian Heritage, The Fourth River, So to Speak: a feminist journal of language and art, New Madrid*, and elsewhere.

Mary Popham is a 2003 graduate of Spalding's Naslund-Mann Graduate School of Writing. Her novels set in Central Kentucky in the early 1900s are *Back Home in Landing Run, The Wife Takes a Farmer*, and *Emmalene of Landing Run*, with a forthcoming title, *Angel of Landing Run*. She leads a writing group, the Cherokee Roundtable; and presents a program, "Writing Your Life Story."

Born on Oahu, **Derek N. Otsuji** is the author of *The Kitchen of Small Hours* (SIU Press, 2021), selected by Brian Turner for the Crab Orchard Poetry Series Open Competition. Recent work has appeared in *32 Poems*, *The Beloit Poetry Journal*, *Bennington Review*, *Crazyhorse*, *Cincinnati Review*, *Southern Review*, and *The Threepenny Review*.

Glen Pourciau's third story collection, *Getaway*, was published in 2021 by Four Way Books. His stories have been published by *AGNI Online*, *Green Mountains Review*, *New England Review*, *New World Writing*, *The Paris Review*, *Post Road*, and others. He lives in Galveston, Texas.

Frances Schenkkan's book *Mr. Stevens' Secretary* about a fictional secretary to Wallace Stevens was a National Poetry Series finalist and was published by the University of Arkansas Press. Her current project, *Whitewash*, is poems in the voice of many personas, including the poet's, about racial division in her hometown of Shreveport and elsewhere.

Based in Louisville, Kentucky, **Alice Gray Stites** serves as Chief Curator, Museum Director for 21c Museum Hotels, a multi-venue contemporary art museum combined with boutique hotels and chef-driven restaurants. Founded by collectors Laura Lee Brown and Steve Wilson, 21c is one of the largest contemporary art museums in the U.S., and North America's only collecting museum dedicated solely to art of the 21st century. Stites curates both solo and group exhibitions that reflect the global nature of art today, as well as site-specific, commissioned installations, and a variety of cultural events at all eight 21c locations.

Katerina Stoykova is the author of several award-winning poetry books in English and Bulgarian, as well as the Senior Editor of Accents Publishing. Her latest book, *Second Skin* (ICU, 2018, Bulgarian) received the Vanya Konstantinova biannual national poetry award, as well as a grant from the European Commission's program Creative Europe for translation and publication in English. Her poems have been translated into German, Spanish, Ukrainian, Bangla, Farsi, and a volume of her selected poems, translated into Arabic by acclaimed poet Khairi Hamdan, was published in Arabic from Dar Al Biruni press in 2022.

J. D. Strunk has a degree in English Literature from the University of Toledo. He has worked as a technical writer in insurance and aerospace, and is currently a copy editor in Denver, Colorado. His fiction has appeared in *Jimson Weed*, *New Plains Review*, and *Conceit Magazine*, and was a finalist for *Bellingham Review*'s Tobias Wolff Award for Fiction.

A Singapore-based writer, editor, storyteller, theatre practitioner and arts educator, **Verena Tay** (www.verenatay.com) has published two collections of short stories and four volumes of plays, as well as edited twelve story anthologies. An Honorary Fellow at the International Writing Program, University of Iowa (Aug–Nov 2007), she was a Writer-in-Residence at Nanyang Technological University (Aug–Nov 2018). She has just completed a PhD in Creative Writing with Swansea University through which she wrote her first novel about three generations of Singaporean Chinese women with a mythological intervention.

Brian Turner has a memoir, *My Life as a Foreign Country*, and two collections of poetry, *Here, Bullet* and *Phantom Noise*, with *The Wild Delight of Wild Things*, *The Goodbye World Poem*, and *The Dead Peasant's Handbook* due out from Alice James Books in Fall, 2023. He's the editor of *The Kiss* and co-edited *The Strangest of Theatres*. He lives in Florida with his dog, Dene, the world's sweetest golden retriever.

Frank X Walker is the author of *A is for Affrilachia*, the forthcoming collection *The Love House Poems*, and 13 other books. He is Professor of English and African American and Africana Studies at the University of Kentucky.

Brookes Washington is a writer and actor. She currently resides in Louisiana and graduated from Nicholls State University with dual degrees in Microbiology and Creative Writing. She is pursuing an MFA in Creative Writing (Fiction) from The University of New Orleans.

Cornerstone Contributors' Notes

Amity Doyle is thirteen years old and a seventh grader living in Katonah, New York. Her previous poems have been published in *The Louisville Review* and *Stone Soup*. She was chosen by judge Billy Collins as a winner of the New York Botanical Gardens Young Poets contest, and her poetry has received a Gold Key from the Scholastic Art & Writing Awards. Amity enjoys writing, dancing, drawing, and singing songs from *Hamilton*.

Emma Catherine Hoff is an eleven-year-old writer and poet from New York City, where she lives with her parents and her cat, Gavroche. Her poems have appeared in the *Rattle Young Poets Anthology*, *The Poetry Society*, *The Louisville Review*, and *Stone Soup Magazine*. Her podcast, *Poetry Soup*, as well as book reviews and essays, appear regularly on the Stone Soup Blog. Her first full poetry collection, *An Archeology of the Future*, won *Stone Soup*'s 2022 Book Contest and will be published in September 2023.

Rihaan Phillip Kapoor recently graduated from eighth grade at St. Francis of Assisi Catholic School in Louisville, Kentucky and will attend Trinity High School in the fall. In addition to writing poetry, he plays tennis, drums, and enjoys competing in science fairs and quick recall matches.

Seth Niemann will be a freshman at DuPont Manual High School in Louisville, Kentucky, after recently graduating from eighth grade at St. Francis of Assisi Catholic School. Seth enjoys playing basketball, volleyball and writing poetry.

Matilda Reinhart graduated from eighth grade at St. Francis of Assisi Catholic High school in Louisville, Kentucky. She will attend Assumption High school. She likes to write, read, and paint along with poem writing. Matilda got the inspiration for her poem from thinking about summer.

John Gabriel Sperl, age 11, is an avid daydreamer and astronomer. He enjoys robotics, reading up on cosmology, building in Minecraft, and designing rockets in Kerbal Space Program. When not immersed in a book, John Gabriel loves to write science-fiction stories and poetry, play the violin, and perform on stage.

Jenny Zhu is a sophomore from Livingston High School in New Jersey. She is an editor and two-year contributor for her school's literary magazine. She enjoys karaoke, cookie dough ice cream, and rainy days.

Alfred Conteh

About the Cover Artist

Alfred Conteh is a multimedia artist living and working in Atlanta, Georgia. His paintings and sculptures have been exhibited and collected by museums across the U.S., including the Amon Carter Museum of American Art, Fort Worth, Texas; the Harvey B Gantt Center for American Art, Charlotte, NC; Minneapolis Institute of Art, Minneapolis, MN; California African American Museum, Los Angeles, CA; Clark Atlanta University Art Museum, Atlanta, Georgia, Smithsonian Library of Congress, Washington, DC, and many others. He is represented by Kavi Gupta Gallery, Chicago, IL and Galerie Myrtis, Baltimore, MD. In October 2023, Conteh will present new work at the Southern Foodways Alliance conference in Oxford, MS, co-commissioned by 21c and SFA.

Merle L. Bachman

Translator's Note

Rosa Nevadovska (1890-1971) was born into a traditional yet worldly Jewish family in Bialystok (Russia). She did not move to America until 1928, when she was thirty-eight years old and had already had a life full of travel, study—and sharp pain, having lost her only child, Leah, to meningitis at the age of two. Like many Jewish immigrants from Eastern Europe, she was faced with the terrible grief of knowing her family, friends and even her home city were destroyed during World War II and the Holocaust. It's not surprising that many of Nevadovska's poems express loneliness and loss, but some also engage a meditative silence amid the anonymity of life in New York City (where she ultimately died). Yet she was also able to tap into joyous moments of transcendence, dating from her years of living near both ocean and desert in Venice, California.

As a translator, I've been drawn to the compressed, emotional quality of Nevadovska's writing. Her poetry, like most written in Yiddish, was built around rhyme. What I've carried over instead are sound echoes and also an attentiveness to the originals' stanzas and line lengths.

With deep thanks to Alice Saitzeff Grossman, literary heir to the works of her aunt, Rosa Nevadovska, for permission to use the Yiddish texts of these poems and to publish my translations.